P9-APR-904

Contents

For Alexandra and Sophia

Graeme Salaman took a BA in Social Sciences in 1965, and a Ph.D. in Industrial Sociology from the University of Cambridge in 1968.

He is currently Senior Lecturer in Sociology at the Open University where he has taken particular interest in, and responsibility for, courses in the sociology of work, and organisations.

He is currently researching the implementation of Equal Opportunities in the London Fire Brigade, and the modernisation of an Indian coal mine (ODA funded). He has published extensively, including: *Community and Occupation* (1974); *People and Organisations* (editor, 1973); *People and Work* (editor, 1975); *Work Organisations, Resistance and Control* (1979); *The Politics of Work and Occupation* (editor, 1980); *Control and Ideology in Organisations* (editor, 1980); *Class and the Corporation* (1982), republished in the USA as *Work Organisations and Class Structure* (1984); *Class at Work* (co-authored with C. Littler, 1984); *Work Culture and Employment* (editor, 1984).

WORKING

GRAEME SALAMAN
Faculty of Social Sciences
The Open University, Milton Keynes

ELLIS HORWOOD LIMITED
Publishers · Chichester

TAVISTOCK PUBLICATIONS
London and New York

First published in 1986 by
ELLIS HORWOOD LIMITED
Market Cross House, Cooper Street,
Chichester, Sussex, PO19 1EB, England
and

TAVISTOCK PUBLICATIONS LIMITED
11 New Fetter Lane, London EC4 4EE

Published in the USA by
TAVISTOCK PUBLICATIONS
and ELLIS HORWOOD LIMITED
in association with METHUEN INC.
733 Third Avenue, New York, NY 10017

© **1986 G. Salaman/Ellis Horwood Limited**

British Library Cataloguing in Publication Data
Salaman, Graeme
Working. — (Key ideas)
1. Industrial sociology
I. Title   II. Series
306'.36   HD6955

ISBN 0–85312–881–2 (Ellis Horwood Limited — Library Edn.)
ISBN 0–85312–920–7 (Ellis Horwood Limited — Student Edn.)

Phototypeset in Times by Ellis Horwood Limited
Printed in Great Britain by R.J. Acford, Chichester

Editor's Foreword

Major change in the economies of the industrialized capitalist societies is forcing a review of the sociology of work. The emphasis on large-scale industry as the paradigmatic form of work organization now appears anachronistic — as does the necessity of a class-based model of society as the context within which to explain social relations in the workplace.

As Graeme Salaman makes clear in this original and highly perceptive essay, the anchoring of the sociology of work in what has come to be known as the 'labour process debate' directs attention to a series of questions which are ultimately restrictive, and away from those which make sense of a wide range of work experiences. Perhaps more importantly, they direct attention away from many of the distinctively social aspects of work organization, towards class and power issues which are highly abstract in form. The main implication is that the experience of work organization for the majority of people is not organized in the class terms that 'labour process' theory would suggest.

It has always been tempting (within the Marxist paradigm) to suggest that people's failure to see their work situation in class terms is 'false consciousness'. Explanations of manifestly exclusionary tactics by one working class group *vis-á-vis* another (e.g. restrictive practices, racism and sexism within particular occupations, etc.) have also drawn upon this device to remain within a perspective that allots primacy to economically defined class as the key variable to explain social and thus work structures. Yet to treat how people structure and understand their work relations as merely examples of ideology or false consciousness when they do not conform to the desired model of working-class solidarity, provides no more than a one-sided picture. It is a way of denying the reality of lived and commonsense experience which may in fact be injurious to the aim of understanding class structuration in capitalist society.

Labour process studies are the direct result of a pioneering book, *Labor and Monopoly Capital* (1974), in which Harry Braverman outlined a thesis which focused on the ways in which management seeks to control the design of work in accordance with the imperatives of capitalism. Such studies have overtaken an earlier tradition of industrial sociology which was concerned with the experience of work, the politics of occupations, and the social or 'community' base of specific occupations and industries. These earlier forms did not of course ignore class dimensions of work structures, but they did not devote as much attention to the distinctive area of concern of the Bravermanians — deskilling. In pointing to the need of management to control the 'labour process' and how work is organized in order to create surplus value which can be extracted from the workforce — Braverman pointed to a key and under-researched area. That this also resonated with the desire to connect concerns with how growing complexity in the organization of work structures could be reconciled with the elegant simplicity of Marx's two-class model of capitalist society perhaps explains the recent dominance of Braverman-inspired perspectives.

Graeme Salaman begins from the position of someone well-versed in the labour process debate. But his concern is to question and explore the recalcitrance of workers in many different work organizations to conform to the Bravermanic precepts. In some ways his work returns to the themes enunciated in the classic Hawthorn factory studies of Roethlisberger and Dickson in the 1930s. But his intentions are fundamentally different. Whereas the Hawthorn studies uncovered the existence of a 'shadow' informal work organization underpinning the formal structure, but saw it as paralleling rather than contesting the latter, Salaman explores the ways in which social relations in the work situation express and define the work group. He provides both a deeper and more textured approach to questions about work-design, as well as analysis of the reasons why the 'labour process' debate ignores key features of the real organization of work.

It is a particularly valuable feature of this book that it draws upon two important empirical studies conducted by Dr Salaman. The distinctive feature of his approach to work relations is its grounding in the careful, perceptive and sensitive observation of particular cases. This is not to imply an inductive methodology on his part — in fact quite the opposite is true — but it does mean that his analyses are alive to the real complexity and multi-layered nature of the work structures he is conceptualizing.

The Key Ideas series is designed to bring thought-provoking writing into the area of the introductory sociology text. This book fulfils such an aim admirably, but also goes further in proposing new directions in the sociology of work. It is tempting to suggest that this little book will constitute a watershed in sociological thinking about work organization, but only time will tell if such an assessment is correct.

Peter Hamilton

Preface

This book makes use of material gathered in the course of two continuing projects — with the London Fire Brigade and the Indian coal sector. Both projects are made use of in this book, used as sources of illustration, for the book is not *about* the London Fire Brigade, or Moonidih mine, but attempts to make some general points about the ways in which social relationships at work are informally structured, and the consequences of these phenomena.

The two studies were conducted under different auspices and circumstances. Both are still in progress. The study of station officers within the London Fire Brigade was carried out as part of an attempt to inform station officers of Equal Opportunities law and policy. Because of the manner in which these discussions were conducted, each discussion with around 10 officers, was encouraged to range widely over issues and problems which they felt aggrieved or confused about. These seminars thus offered a major opportunity to learn from the officers as well as to argue the merits of law and policy. The analysis presented here was based on approximately 25 such discussions held over a period of three years.

The analysis of the response to new coal-getting equipment in an Indian Coal mine was initially funded by research funds from the Open University, which allowed a visit to India to establish the basic facts of the modernization programme and to gather data on its reception and impact. Following this visit, an application was made to the Overseas Development Administration, which department is responsible for funding the modernization programme, and this application being successful, research has started in India and the UK, with visits to Department of Coal, Delhi, Coal India Ltd., Calcutta, the Central Mine Planning and Design Institute, Ranchi, Bihar, and Moonidih mine, and Bharat Coking Coal, Ltd., Bihar, as well as to British manufacturers and mining consultants.

A number of people helped me with access to, and understanding of, the two case studies. I would like to acknowledge their help and support;

M. S. Gujral, Jim Savage, Bill Chambers, R. K. Sachdev, Professor Ashok Desai, Dr. Bharat Bhushan, Robbie Patterson, Dr. M. M. Seam, A. K. Sahay, Dr. Sean Conlin, Tricia Tierney, Nandita Haksar, Dr. G. Alam, Alan Weeks, Dr Partha Ghose, Tony Connoly, Charmian Houselander, D. O. David Cartwright, D.O. Ken Gordon, and David Wainwright. None of these people has the slightest responsibility for the analyses that follow. They may even disagree with them. The content of the book and its arguments are my responsibility alone.

Introduction

Let us imagine that we can start afresh and design a new sociology of work as if we were blissfully ignorant of what are currently regarded as the important issues and questions within this area of enquiry. Obviously such a savage depletion would constitute a very considerable absence. But, at least hypothetically it would force us to recognize two related truths: that the existing body of writing in the sociology of work has the consequence of effectively limiting the issues which are regarded as constituting the proper subject matter of analysis; and secondly, that freedom from such work would allow us to consider afresh just what should, or could be, the subject matter of a sociological approach to work. As things stand we possibly stand too much in awe of existing debates, not able to see beyond the parameters of the currently fashionable approach, or problematic.

In short, in as much as the current sociology of work represents an attempt, or a series of attempts, to come up with some answers, they are answers to a limited series of questions. Questions and answers go together, after a time establishing a dialogue of such dominance as to drown the possibility of other queries, or even masking the fact that a particular series of problems has assumed an unwarranted degree of legitimacy.

This small book may then be seen as an attempt to raise some alternative, if highly traditional questions — questions which may in fact even have benefit for the existing conventions of the sociology of work. There is no alternative approach being offered here; rather suggestions for some issues which could merit further analysis and some suggestions for ways in which these issues might be approached.

But to return to our hypothetically bereft sociology of work, if we were to answer the question, 'What is the sociology of work?', not by reference to what currently, or even historically is regarded as the sociology of work, but in terms of what such a form of enquiry could, or should be like, then we might well find that a such an 'ideal' sociology of work would include a much wider range of problems and approaches than those currently in vogue. Ideally, naively even, a sociology of work would seek to explain the social aspects of work by reference to social causes. Since all forms of work — even those that occur individually, or privately, or even surreptitiously — have a social element in that they occur within a context of work, or services created or performed for others, often under the control of others in forms and contexts and under conditions established by others (i.e. socially), it is possible to say that the most striking feature of work, wherever it is performed — whether housework in industrial Britain, or canoe building in Melanesia — is precisely its social character. All forms of human work are highly, and systematically socially organized. It is this essentially social character of work which sociology should seek to describe and explain, bearing in mind that the social patterning of work must be understood in the widest possible sense to include how work is patterned and organized, rewarded and evaluted, controlled and recruited. In particular, as this book will argue, a sociological approach would, quite simply, seek to understand what goes on at work — the whole complex mesh of social work processes. This point won't be laboured here; it is made simply to distinguish a whole-hearted approach to the sociological enterprise from a particular, even parochial version which may be in the ascendant at any one time, and to suggest the rich, ambitious possibilities of this endeavour, which will be described below. For this book is an attempt to restore or revive some of the forgotten questions whose current dismissal impoverishes the sociological endeavour and may even weaken its explanatory power.

The organization of the book is as follows. Chapter 1 spells out the basic elements of the current vogue within the sociology of work. This 'problematic' (for each method of approach is centred around a major 'problem' which it is designed to resolve) is not critiqued here; that has been done enough elsewhere; our intention is neither to bury nor to praise, but simply to identify the costs of a particular approach in terms of the 'opportunity costs' — the questions which aren't asked because others are. This chapter will the proceed to outline in a very general way the approach being advocated in this book: the study of relationships at work. We intend to execute this with sufficient thoroughness to make the following chapter, which contains two case studies, comprehensible. But detailed analysis of the analysis of social relations at work must wait until Chapter 4. Chapters 2 and 3 then contain the two major case studies of the book: analyses of the apparent resistance of station officers in the London Fire Brigade to the application of Equal Opportunities legislation and Brigade equal opportunities policy, and of the claimed failure of the modernization of some mines in the Indian coal sector. We shall consider one mine: Moonidih mine, part of Bharat Coking Coal Ltd., Bihar, which has recently received power face equipment from British manufacturers, with Overseas Development

Administration finance. As indicated. Chapter 4 will then review the ways in which social relationships at work have been treated in the literature. In this chapter our review of earlier studies will take us from corrupt police-men to 'indulged' gypsum miners to factory workers' bantering. The intention of this chapter is to sketch the richness and the variety of the ways in which the traditional sociology of work has treated and conceptualized — and explained — social relations at work. Chapter 5 then advances a model of social relations at work, being an attempt to classify and categorize what seem to be the major axes of differentiation and causation of social relations.

1

The labour process and work relations

We start with a brief description of the current state of the sociology of work, and then proceed to a more general, traditional form of sociological enquiry in which we establish the characteristic foci of interest, and characteristic approach of the type of sociological enquiry adopted here and conclude by noting that current forms of sociological investigation of currently fashionable problematics actually founder because of their very failure to address the wider issues of social relations at work.

Current forms of sociological interest in work stem from the 1974 publication of Harry Braverman's *Labor and Monopoly Capital*. This book marked the onset of sweeping Bravermania. The essentials of this condition are as follows: first, a concern to investigate the relationship between the imperatives of capitalism as these impinge on those who own and those who manage work corporations; second a conviction — well-supported empirically — that a major aspect of this relationship is the necessity for management to take responsibility for the design of work, and to design work in accordance with the basic precepts of Scientific Management, or Taylorism (see Littler (1982) for a very clear statement of these principles). Essentially, Taylorism involves the fragmenting and de-skilling of work, in order to achieve increased output from a more manageable and cheaper (because less skilled and less trained) workforce.

It would be hard to overestimate the importance and influence of these arguments, constituting, as they do, a forceful restatement in modern terms, of the arguments of Marx's *Capital*, Volume 1. It is greatly to Braverman's credit that he reasserted the relevance and significance of sociological — and political and practical — interest in the origin of work forms, and in particular in the relationship between Capitalism, as a form of economy which revolves around the necessity for management to design and to redesign work in order to achieve satisfactory, competitive levels of return on investment, and the design of work and, indeed, technology. As Giddens remarks: 'Braverman shows that the rationality of technique in modern industrial enterprise is not neutral in respect of class domination . . . if Braverman's argument is correct, industrial technique embodies the capital/wage-labour relation in its very form' (Giddens, 1982, p. 39).

Post-Braverman, critical interest in the issues he raised has tended to focus somewhat partially on his work, 'interpreting' it in ways which Braverman himself, had he survived the publication of his work, might have resisted. Two major areas of interest, theoretical conceptual and empirical, have emerged: de-skilling and strategies of control. De-skilling assumes importance because it is seen, *pace* Braverman, as representing the necessary form or tendency, of work design within capitalism, Empirical investigations of this tendency thus become, in essence, 'tests' of the thesis itself. Strategies of control attract attention because Braverman is conventionally read as having offered a theory of the necessity for capital to control the workforce to ensure complicance with whatever requirements the imperatives of competitive profitability demand. There are various aspects to this interpretation of Braverman.

First, it can be said that by having reasserted the class aspects of relationships between management and workforce Braverman succeeds in defining workplace relations between workers and management in class terms, and thus places the requirement of control of one class (management) over another (workers) as central to the deployment of the workforce in activities which will produce profitable levels of output for management.

Secondly, once workplace relations are defined as class relations, workers not only need to be controlled, i.e. directed, they also need to be monitored and supervised, since they are, definitionally, untrustworthy, as members of an opposed class.

Thirdly, because relations between management and workforce are class relations, management will need constantly to seek ways of undermining, or obstructing, or overwhelming, workers' (class) resistance.

In terms of these post-Braverman foci of interest, then, it is not surprising that the concept of management strategies of control has assumed considerable importance. This concept is used in a number of ways, sometimes emphasizing the design of organization structure itself ('strategic choice', see Child (1973)), sometimes focusing on industrial relations strategies to weaken unions, divide unions, win allegiance from union to management, etc., sometimes looking at the design of work itself, or more commonly, at the manipulation of the employment relationship. This latter concept needs amplification and we shall proceed to this below. But here it should be remarked that the notion of management strategy of control in all or any of its forms, represents a major current post-Braverman focus of interest. This is because, in the event that actual workplace relations appeared to be more complex than Braverman initially suggested, and in the event that management does not always, apparently, seek to achieve control through one, monolithic means (Taylorism and deskilling) the overall thesis that capitalism has definite consequences for management's need to control workers in order to ensure an obedient, compliant and cheap workforce is saved by the argument that the precise way in which management will seek to achieve this control will vary under varying circumstances, not least of which is the response of the workforce to the earlier strategy of control. This serial model of control is particularly evident in Edward's influential book *Contested Terrain* (1979), where each new form of control is seen to 'solve' the problems of the earlier form, but only at the cost of introducing new problems which in turn require further developments. Forms of control, Edwards argues, change as a result of 'the continuing contention of classes, the struggle of capitalists, workers, and others to protect and advance their interests' (Edwards, 1979, p. viii). The 'Labour Process debate' (as the discussion of the issues raised by Braverman is known) demonstrates an uncertainty, a collective hesitation when dealing with the issues of de-skilling and control. The uncertainty is of this form: Braverman argued that capitalism generated one classic form of work — Taylorism — which articulated in clear and classic form the requirements of work under capitalism: cheapness, control and transferability.

This argument is clear, strong and unequivocal. The trouble is that it is also wrong. Work under capitalism takes a much greater variety of forms. De-skilling is not universal, may not be even an increasing tendency; control can be achieved in many other ways. So much has been noted and argued by many writers within the Labour Process debate, (for example, see the collection edited by Stephen Wood, *The Degradation of Work* 1982). It is thus conventional to save Braverman from himself, as it were, by noting that he placed excessive emphasis on one form of work design and one method of control within capitalism, whereas in fact capitalism displays a greater variety of forms of work and control, which represent in different ways management's efforts to achieve its objectives under changing conditions, including, crucially, the responses of the workforce.

This rescue operation, however, actually undermines the basic model rather seriously; if, within capitalism, there is a variety of work forms, then what factors determine the transition from one form to another? What are the broad historical tendencies within capitalist work organizations? This salvaging of Braverman from the historical and empirical inaccuracy of his major claims weakens the basic thesis by eliminating the original, simple and unmediated connection between capitalism and work (the latter representing the 'general law of the capitalist division of labour'). This has the merit of simplicity: capitalism=Taylorism. And those who argue for a more contingent relationship must adduce a more complex and variable intervening mechanism, whereby variations in capitalism, or features of management or of worker knowledge, attitude, strategy, result in a particular form of work design or control strategy. For now the link is no longer a necessary one: it can be realized in a number of ways (some presumably as yet unknown or untried). Thompson correctly remarks;

> The fact that the dictates of accumulation require control of the labour process by capital does not tell us what form of control will be applicable in different circumstances. Nor does it distinguish between management choices based on considerations of short- and long-term profitability. No one has convincingly demonstrated that a particular form of control is necessary or inevitable for capitalism to function successfully. (Thompson, 1985, p. 151)

A major consequence of this introduction of various 'mediating' variables in the connection between capitalism and work design or control strategy is in effect to introduce a new concept of class. We have seen that Braverman's analysis depends on class as a form of capitalist dynamic, whereby capital must constantly seek to design work to the ends of greater competitive advantage, which has the consequence of efforts to redefine the exchange of wages for workers' efforts in managments' advantage (see Littler and Salaman, 1984). Furthermore we have seen that class is also used to describe relationships between workers and management as the latter constantly seek to control, direct, and supervise the former. Even work technology itself, as the remarks of Giddens argue, now becomes an aspect of class relations.

But the introduction of the concept of management strategy introduces a new sense in which class may be used: in terms of the development of class consciousness and class solidarity. After all, by introducing the notion of strategy, management attitudes, knowledge, intentions become crucial, and so too do worker attitudes, responses, objectives. In short, once the mechanical, functional (see Salaman, 1982) relationship between capitalism and work is broken, then management knowledge, competence, consciousness, become part of the causal chain — necessary steps in the relationship between capitalism and work forms. Similarly, the attitudes, solidarity, perceptions, strategies of the workforce become equally crucial.

This development of the argument introduces what is, essentially, the key issue in class theory: the 'structuration' of classes, i.e. the extent to which, and manner in which, economic categories become real, social categories and the basis of experienced interests (see Giddens, 1980). Braverman himself, for example, in his treatment of management consciousness, shifts between viewing managers as omniscient conspirators, constantly and actively seeking to degrade labour, and a view of management as mere cyphers, reflexively responding to capitalism's needs. Such an approach leaves little space for the investigation of those factors which actually influence management - or workforce — attitudes and decision-making; nor do they permit the analysis of the nature and content of management — or workforce — ideas, values, or myths. As in Weber, but less explicitly, these theories operate with a form of workplace rationality. But unlike Weber's, these theories fail to acknowledge — possibly even to realize — that their conception of key subjects' knowledge, values and objectives are highly idealized, insufficiently explored, and simply regarded as the equivalents, reflections, of class position. As Richard Brown has recently remarked 'one consequence of this form of over-determined analysis and explanation is that . . . overdetermined views of human history and society leave no room for and assign no weight to individual, group, experience, meaning and action: structure predominates over agency' (Brown, 1984, p. 317).

The treatment of worker subjectivity is similarly flawed: on occasion worker subjectivity is assumed to be in a state of constant potential class consciousness and resistance which is never finally realized because of the artful strategies of obfuscation and division developed by management; and while elsewhere other writers acknowledge actual patterns of worker action and organization and seek empirically to assess their role in influencing work design, there is relatively little attention paid to the systematic, workplace determinants of workers' viewpoints. Workers too are seen passively, passively accepting and being duped by, management strategies.

The analysis and focus of this book suggests some of the ways in which this passive conception of workers and managers may be replaced by an approach which regards both, and all forms of employees, as engaged in active efforts to make sense of, and to a degree achieve control over, their work destinies and experience. Frequently these 'rationalities' have little to do with formal managerial views, or with sociological expectations of class-based consciousnesses. Nevertheless these 'rationalities' do make sense to those involved in them, and are accessible to sociological analysis, if not via the concepts of Bravermania. Yet it is increasingly obvious that the labour process must begin to take seriously a level of analysis and explanation which is not apparently amenable to the concepts promulgated within that debate as it stands.

The Labour Process debate, in its recent discussions, which perforce, developed and depended upon the notion of management strategy to cope with the apparent variety of forms of work and control and the variety of types of actual relationship between management and workforce, has been required to rely on a relatively unexplored notion of class consciousness, organization, solidarity and action. The debate thus centres on a critical sociological — and social — problem: the problem of class structuration.

However, certain writers have recently suggested some necessary elements of a satisfactory approach to this question. First, Penn (1985) has sensibly argued that the issue of class structuration — the emergence of classes as social collectivities — is a matter not for dogmatic assertion but of investigation. Writing of the conventional approach to class attitudes which, having defined classes in some theoretically derived ways, then searches for evidence of appropriate forms and levels of consciousness among those who can be classified as members of the relevant classes, and explains any discrepancy between class and attitude in terms of mediating, obscuring factors, Penn notes that this form of analysis 'puts the cart before the horse. In particular, there appears to be an assumption that the working class has existed or exists in some sort of pristine fashion. The main purpose of this research is to investigate the nature and existence of the working class, not to assume it' (Penn, 1985, pp. 12–13).

As Penn notes, the work of Giddens referred to earlier offers much help here, particularly Giddens's suggestions for the factors which he terms sources of mediate and proximate structuration. These refer to those variables which influence the development of classness and include the closure on mobility, thus restricting social relationships to those who share market capacity of some sort, the division of labour, authority relations within the firm and the influence of distributive groupings (Giddens, 1982, p. 160). It will be clear — and it will be discussed later in this book — that these factors listed by Giddens usefully summarize those variables responsible for shared experiences of a class sort, i.e. experience of subordination, of work, of inequalities of level of reward.

However, if we are interested in classes as groups with a consciousness of shared interests then it is clear that 'groups do not share interests simply because they occupy the same or similar place in the division of labour . . . classes are formed through the experience of common struggle' (Sabel, 1982, p. 18). And this leads us back to an issue which was raised earlier but not fully explored: the employment relationship.

The employment relationship refers to the arrangement whereby workers agree to offer their willingness to work to the limits of their strength, knowledge and skill for an employer for a limited number of hours for a level of remuneration. Exactly what the employer offers varies not only in amount, but in the number and variety of rewards on offer (see

Littler and Salaman, 1984, and Dunkerley and Salaman, 1986). It has been argued, (for example by Cohen, 1986) that in fact the employer under capitalism is necessarily concerned with the manipulation of the wage/effort exchange — which constitutes the heart of the employment relationship — such that unit costs fall, or output increases. Cohen argues that Braverman's thesis is not that the capitalist requires control per se, but that s/he is necessarily forced constantly to seek more effort, or more output, from the employees. The issue over which conflict occurs then is not the question of control per se, but the question of intensity and levels of output, and the levels at which they are rewarded. Support for this argument is available in figures on causes of strikes, which confirm that the vast mass of strikes are occasioned by disputes over pay, or over pay-related issues.

Now, if the employment relationship is a critical factor in determining relations between management and workers (who differ markedly precisely in terms of how their efforts are rewarded, and indeed in the way in which performance is measured (see, for example, Taylor (1982) and his discussion of management salaries and 'perks'), then it is critical that workers are themselves significantly differentiated in terms of employment conditions. So marked are these differences that many writers have referred to them as constituting a segmentation of the labour market into two sorts of job: primary and secondary. These sorts of jobs are characterized by markedly different employment terms. Primary jobs are secure, well-paid, with pleasant conditions and security. Secondary jobs are poorly paid, done under arduous conditions and are insecure, often casual, or part-time (see, for example, Garnsey *et al.,* (1985) and Rubery (1978)). Now this segmentation of jobs raises two interesting issues. First, the effect of these differences is to divide the workforce, to create differences of experience and differences of attitude and consciousness. This effect is enormously enhanced when the differences in question coincide with other significant social divisions — of age, of gender and of race. We shall return to this point later, for this is a crucial factor in affecting the development of class consciousness and class interests and is a good example of the central theme of this book: the significance of relationships at work in the structuring of work processes, and events.

Secondly, the origins of these differences between jobs also demonstrate the role of existing patterns of relationships in mediating the development of class structures. Rubery for example has argued cogently that although many authors regarded these job differences in terms of management strategies to divide and rule the workforce, or as efforts to create a stable and skilled workforce, in fact these job demarcations — while they may be at the expense of working-class homogeneity — can also be to the benefit of those incumbents of primary sector jobs who are able to secure and retain advantage. Rubery remarks:

> Workers' defence against competition in the labour market is to organise to control the supply of labour. Attempts may be made at the macro level to limit the supply of new types of labour, such as females or immigrants. More importantly, workers will organise to control entry into an occupation, firm or industry. Such control must be to the detriment of groups excluded from the organised sectors as it reduces their mobility and may even increase competition in the external labour market. (Rubery, 1978, p. 29)

To summarize the preceding discussion, and to point its relevance for our discussion: the major debate within the sociology of work — one which is so dominant as to swamp alternative agenda — consists of an exploration of the relationship between capitalism and work design and work technology and control at work. The original seminal contribution to this debate argued a relatively simplistic and empirically vulnerable relationship between capitalism and work which has been succeeded by an emphasis on management strategies under capitalism as managers seek to achieve their various class objectives. This formulation of the theory, however, depends considerably on the class consciousness, activity, organization, solidarity of categories of employees as members of classes. The evidence suggests that such classness cannot by any means be assumed but must be investigated. Such analyses of the factors which result in class structuration show the importance of other patterns of social relationships in consolidating, or dividing, workers into class groups. Of particular significance is the way in which workers — and indeed managers — compete against each other, against a backdrop of capitalist dynamics and pressures. The point to be emphasized at this stage of our discussion is that a theory of work structure and process which explains these in terms of class relations is nevertheless required to incorporate, at a crucial stage of the argument, non-class workplace relations, whose only connection with class is that they occur within a class context and that they play a part in determining class structuration. Nevertheless in their own terms they are not class relations (relations between men and women, white and black, skilled and unskilled, young and old).

Since a major focus of this book is on the significance of workplace relations in explanations of work processes and structures and events, we can take the necessary inclusion of such factors, even in a form of theory which is not *prima facie* sympathetic to our emphasis on the significance of work relations generally, as a strongly supporting sign. But this leaves the major issue: what exactly do we mean by workplace relations? What sort of work processes and structures are they able to explain? It is to these questions that we now turn.

WORKPLACE RELATIONS

When we refer to workplace relations and argue their significance for an understanding of work structures and processes and events, it should be emphasized that this is not to offer a theory of work. The Labour Process debate does offer a theory of work structures and work processes in that it seeks to explain what happens at work — or selection of some events that are defined as significant, i.e. the design of work and control — in terms of class and class dynamics. Within this view social relations at work are indeed critical, but only in as much as these are defined as class relations. However, as we have seen, ironically, the manifestation of classes and class relationships is constantly subject to obstruction because of other patterns of social relationship which undermine or cross-cut class allegiances and thus obscure the development of class interests.

In this book, however, we cast our net wider; we do not start with any preconceived conviction as to the origins, nature or causes of patterns of relationships at work. We shall in fact try to advance a general approach which includes a wide variety of structures and their causes and origins. Nor do we assert in advance the necessary class nature of such patterns. They may signify classes, they may be fractions of classes, they may be entirely distinct from, or even antithetical to, the formation of classes. These are empirical questions, to be investigated, not assumed. What this book will try to do is to identify the complex ways in which within work organizations, structures of loyalty and estrangement, identification and rejection, trust and distrust, and shared viewpoints against opposed viewpoints, can build up on various bases and under various conditions.

What is being offered here then is not a theory of work, although most theories of work include as a central feature a theory of work relationships (see, for example, Salaman (1982)) but an argument that if the sociological study of work is defined rather more broadly than it is by the post-Braverman debate, to include a concern to understand not simply the origins of work forms and control methods — crucial though these questions be — but also other aspects of work structure and process, then it becomes essential to address attention to the way in which relationships at work are patterned, the consequences of such patterning, and bases on which they can develop, for very frequently the explanation of what goes on within organizations can be mounted in terms of these structures.

When we refer to wider problematics than those offered by the Labour Process debate we don't wish to downgrade these critical concerns but simply to suggest that they be seen as simply one set among a number of possible sets of interesting questions. It is also interesting, for example, to ask: why are some business organizations much more efficient than others? Or, why are members of some public organizations consistently corrupt? Or, why is a particular technology effective in one context and not in another? Or, what happens when an organization seeks to install and implement an Equal Opportunities programme? These are not the sort of questions that the Labour Process debate would address. Within that theory these are epiphenomenal, sideshows. Yet they are interesting questions, socially and often personally important questions, and quite definitely, sociological questions. They are also questions among many others that require us to explore the patterning of workplace relationships.

What do we mean by workplace relations? First it must be stressed that, at least in employed work, relations are formally and explicitly structured. This is what organization means: that how people relate, on what issues, in what ways, are carefully designed; that, for example, incumbents of some organizational roles are formally charged with authority and responsibility to allocate work, check quality, monitor discipline and time-keeping etc. of other people. Of course this and other authority is hedged about with restrictions stemming from managment policy, union–management agreements, government legislation (Health and Safety, Equal Opportunties). Nevertheless even these restrictions constitute in their own way another formalization and specification of work relationships.

The major features of the structure of work organizations are also the main axes along which work relationships are patterned. Organizational structure involves horizontal differentiation (departments, areas of work etc.) and vertical differentiation as one person or one level or section takes responsibility for the work of other, subordinate people and departments. These are the major axes along which relations are organized: relations within are severely different from relationships between levels and department in intensity frequency and, most of all, significance. We shall return to this point in later chapters.

Formally speaking as far as those responsible for organizational structure and design are concerned (and for those brands of sociological theory which take a highly 'rational' view of work organizations) this structuring of relationships at work is regarded as functional for the organization's efficient pursuit of its objectives. There are a number of obvious difficulties with this argument, as Silverman points out (1970). First, organization consist of many people and, as we have seen, many levels and departments. How then can we talk unproblematically of an organization's goals as if these were straightforward and uniform and homogeneous? Clearly, while at the formal level there may be a public, stated goal enshrined in company statements and shareholders' brochure (or governors' declarations, or Trustees' . . .), this should not be taken to distract attention from the probability that a variety of actual goals are being pursued within the organization (see Salaman 1979).

Secondly, as anyone with any experience of work organizations knows very well there is a world of difference between what is meant to happen within places of work and what actually goes on. The first thing the new recruit to a place of work does it to 'learn the rules' — the informal practices, short-cuts, gossip, myths, fiddles. As the eager recruit anxiously approaches his or her first jobs and responsibilities s/he is told in the memorable and comforting preamble to some recipe for survival: 'Oh, you don't want to bother with that . . . what we do is like this . . .'.

Certainly places of work contain formal rules and procedures and structures; whether these actually reflect work practices will be determined by the results of the coming together of formal requirements and actual problems, actual patterns of social relationships. To say that the formal equals organizationally effective, while the informal is somehow aberrant and inefficient, is misleading. What is necessary is to consider the actual pay-offs of patterns of behaviour for all the parties involved in terms of their actual work pressures, their work knowledge and their work objectives, and to investigate their actual consequences, rather than to preempt the outcome by labelling them deviant, irrational, 'false-consciousness'. By a grotesque irony the theoretically inclined industrial sociologist can join the moralizing manager in bemoaning the irrationality of employees' views, their naivety in accepting and holding irrational views.

Formal organizational control over work relationships is considerable, but is not complete, and indeed is not the only form of control — there is also informal control, as we shall see. However, formal control takes three forms: control over direction (who is the employee allowed to relate to?), control over the content of relationships (what form are relationships allowed to take?), and the criteria properly to be used when making organizational decisions (why choices and decisions are made). We shall briefly consider each of these.

Formally, organization structure closely specificies the direction of relationships by stipulating to whom each employee should properly relate. For example, foremen have precise instructions about to whom their authority applies and to whom it is quite inapplicable. Members of the services, hospital doctors, station officers in Fire Brigades, head teachers all know (although they may still choose to reject) the organizational personnel who fall within their authority, those with whom they should, as equals, liaise, and those under whose authority they fall. Mistakes in this area are serious. As an organizational employee one is, willy-nilly, an incumbent of a position, one of the main features of which, apart from the work tasks associated with it, is a body of other organizational members with whom one has close, but varied, working contact (known sometimes as the 'role-set'). Relations with these others are closely specified. Furthermore, relationships outside these specified associates, seniors, subordinates, equals, may be difficult, or actively constrained. In some cases, employees are strongly discouraged from any relationships other than those formally directed. Managers, and army officers, for example, in Britain, if not elsewhere, very often have separate eating, recreation and toilet facilities, presumably on the grounds that, within British class culture, 'familiarity breeds contempt'. Worker are often unable to communicate with their fellows because of the ambient noise, or the sheer speed of the line. Early in the industrial period, employers were very concerned indeed to control and discipline the socializing of their workforce. Sexual relations of any sort were a particular focus of attention, possibly because of their obvious potential for disruption. Relationships are not only directed then, they are also forbidden.

But the *content* of these relationships is also regulated. Few supervisors, mercifully, have power of life and death over employees. Even the fiercest sergeant-major has limits on the proper exercise of his authority, and members of all positions know not only to whom they must formally relate, but how they should relate: the limits of their authority, the extent of their rights, the nature of the other's expectations. Any job which involves authority over others involves, definitionally, a job description specifying the nature and the limits of that authority.

Finally, the criteria by which work decisions should be taken are also specified. Ideally, these should be quite impersonal, technical, objective, arrived at purely through the application of rules — bureaucratic or technical. The outcome of bureaucratic or technical decisions should not be affected by subjective, partisan factors. It should stay the same regardless of who fills the organizational role. As noted, some writers have argued that this model of work organization structure and functioning is necessary for efficiency (for example Weber (1964), although his apparent connection of bureaucratic 'rationality' and efficiency has been questioned, for example by Albrow (1970)). However, other writers, some of whose work is discussed in Chapter 4, have argued that (a) this model is not necessarily efficient, and is in fact cumbersome and unresponsive (see for example the discussion of these authors in Salaman (1979)), and (b) that informal patterns of relationships are quite possibly equally effective, offering, as they do a more flexible, and more participative method of working. We must also remember the point made earlier that it is not possible to talk of notions of efficiency without raising the query: efficient for whom? There is clearly not necessarily, not usually, just one shared organizational goal.

These formal requirements are not necessarily a description of what actually happens in organizations. Some sergeant-majors *are* monsters, and get away with it; some workers bully their foreman; some managers have much more influence than their formal position would indicate. The final actual outcome of organizational structure and process is a negotiated outcome between formal requirements and specifications and other, informal pressures. Whether the end result leans towards the preferences of one group or another is of course an issue decided by internal bargaining and power.

There are many studies which illustrate this. Penn (1985) for example shows that workers' capacity to protect themselves from de-skilling initiatives of management is not simply a result of their 'skill' levels, for skills themselves are socially constructed. He argues that 'what is central to, and crucial for, the success of these sectional organizations of skilled manual workers in their struggles to preserve their exclusive controls over work processes has been their strong organization and the relatively weak (from the perspective of bargaining) structure of local capitalist employers or, in other words, the nature of the local labour market' (Penn, 1985, p. 133). Numerous other studies, many of them discussed in Salaman (1979), document the same point: that the outcome of internal negotiations about the relative supremacy of managment direction or employee resistance is a function of the relative power of the two parties, and thus, essentially of the degree to which the employees have managed to achieve some control over a process or problem critical to management — have obtained some control over uncertainty. The issue is a complex one. Certainly it cannot be argued that intra-organizational informal power is simply a consequence of class position. The situation is much more contradictory than this. For example, one often finds that management attempts to resolve a problem by establishing new, clear and ostensibly highly rational procedures, actually makes matters worse by disturbing existing and traditional balances between interested parties. Or such innovations may set up new alliances and clusterings which to some degree oppose or resist the logic and clusterings which to some degree oppose or resist the logic and thrust of the proposed change.

In numerous ways the informal structures of work organizations play a highly significant role in the mediating of actual organizational behaviour and structures. We shall consider two cases of this collision of formal, rational innovation with the cultures and practices of entrenched informal structures in the following two chapters. A classic example of this sort of paradoxical outcome to management initiative is when management learns that shopfloor employees are consistently breaking some safety rule, or are 'pilfering' materials. Horrified, management insist that first line management 'tighten up' on the misdemeanour. But things begin to get worse, conflicts break out, morale suffers, the foremen come under attack, goodwill is withdrawn. What probably has happened is that a delicate balance of forces whereby foremen allowed a measure of indulgency with respect to the breaking of some rule which everyone 'knew' was unimportant or silly or unjust, in exchange for a measure of general compliance, has been totally overthrown. The result: chaos. (For a fascinating illustration of this see Gouldner (1954).)

Finally it is necessary briefly to spell out the major elements of workplace social relationships and to indicate the reasons for their claimed explanatory significance.

Workplace relations have three key characteristics: concerning the social, the normative and issues of personal identity. We shall deal with each in turn.

Workplace relations are, as will be clear from the preceding discussion, patterned. That is, employees interact more frequency, and with greater intimacy, with some fellow-employees than they do with others. The bases of the demarcations that pattern work relationships are, as we have seen, various, sometimes originating in formal specifications, more frequently being a composite, compromise response to the meeting of formal and informal. Whatever the origins of these social isobars, their connection with issues of power, negotiation and conflict is clear: being able to resist formal specifications is a result of interests and solidarity which emerge from the social cohesion of the resisting category, as the remarks of Penn quoted earlier illustrate. Secondly, the likelihood of such centres of *potential* resistance being able to develop is, at least to some degree, a function of the success of management efforts to divide and differentiate the workforce — for example, by the introduction of new technology, requiring less skill, and being worked part-time by a female workforce. In other words we may identify a tension between formal and informal aspects of organizations — that is the uneasy relationship between emergent, often partial, 'grass-roots' structuring of workplace relations (with the three elements mentioned above) which can only be achieved by a degree of control and exclusion, and official, policy-based requirements and rulings. Frequently the meeting of these two elements produces a degree of fragile compromise. A compromise which is necessary to the continued operation of the total organization as it is. We may also recognize a similar distinction, also carrying suggestions of tension, between bases of differentiation and integration. Indeed work organizations can sensibly be seen as phenomena which experience constant and contrary impulses towards *differentiation* (formal attempts to design work, allocate responsibilities; 'informal' attempts by groups of employees to protect themselves, achieve a degree of self-control, separate themselves from others and achieve some 'shelter') and *integration* (management attempts to insist on the truth of their conception of the enterprise as an integrated 'family', team, organic unit; employees' efforts to establish broad-based solidarity to resist, formally, management encroachments on employees' interests). The resulting structuring of a work organization is a consequence of some balance — impossible to predict in advance — of these centripetal and centrifugal forces.

However, it should not be thought that the only or prime axis of social differentiation is the management/shop-floor divide. One of the main points of this book is to consider the complexity of this division, and the myriad bases which may develop on which can grow informal structuring of various sorts. Alliances across the management/shop-floor line, particularly incorporating lower management in shop-floor relationships, and divisions within management or within the frequently not homogeneous shop-floor are common. So are divisions within each of these major camps. These will be discussed in Chapter 4.

Workplace relations are patterned, then, such that frequency, intimacy and the significance of contacts are not distributed equally, or haphazardly, but follow certain describable paths. This differentiation is not simply a descriptive fact: it is highly significant to those involved. It is seen as the ways things are, and should be. It is a subject of a workplace morality. Relations, it could be said, are characterized by a pattern of social differentiation — of identified and celebrated differences — and sometimes, but not always, of active, purposeful, social exclusion, based on a number of different identifying features regarded, by the insiders, as critical. Freedman, for example, identifies this phenomenon and relates it firmly to a strategy of risk reduction whereby employees seek to develop a 'shelter' from the vicissitudes of market-based job insecurities:

> In the labor market, maximizing group interest and minimizing risk rest on exclusion, which may be justified on the grounds that people are not members of certain associations, that they lack credentials or seniority, or that their age, sex or race is inappropriate. Whatever the particular exclusionary mode, the purpose is to constitute barriers to entry into preferred occupations. (Freedman, 1984, p. 57)

Certainly this is a *common* basis for the structuring of social relationships. But it is not by any means the only one; this is an issue to which we return in

Chapters 4 and 5. It is revealing and typical that Freedman sees such essential aspects of informal workplace structures entirely in terms of their *purpose* of achieving exclusion. Certainly this is a key element in the phenomenon, as we shall see. But it is not clear that this is an explicit purpose of the informal organization of work relations. Characteristically Freedman's interest in these structures is in their potential or role as sources of class-relevant struggles for advantage. They may play this role. They may potentially be capable of playing this role. But they may not.

We are interested in the category of employees who are differentiated from others (or certain others) and among whom there is a frequency and a significance of social interaction. This is a looser form of social organization, for example, than that described by the term group (although it certainly also includes that form of relationship), and it involves a close level of interaction among members who are personally known to each other. Our object of analysis may subsume groups, but is not coterminous with groups. It is not necessary for all members of a category of employees to know each other personally and to relate all together for the processes we are considering here to occur. The effective patterning of relations is looser than a pure group structure (see, for example Homans, 1961) relationships are characterized by shared values, intimacy, a culture, of a limited sort. Relations within a category of employees of this sort are characterized by a degree of trust. This is important because, as we shall see later, the existence of trust, or of distrust, is a crucially important factor in understanding workplace events. Relations within the category are defined differently and experienced differently from relations with outsiders. (The notions 'insiders', 'outsiders', 'us' and 'them' are central to the phenomenon.) This doesn't mean that relations within are by any means necessarily relations of friendship or even marked solidarity. It is possible for one of the values of such a social structuring to be cautious individualism, as amongst the Fire Service officers discussed in the next chapter. But whatever the particular content of the values which accompany the structuring of relations, these will be experienced as having a greater degree of intensity than relations outside, and will be seen as reflecting a similarity, which is in marked contrast to the important differences displayed by outsiders. The precise nature of these identified differences will vary and cannot be predicted without knowledge of the situation and the basis on which the demarcation of relationships occurs. What can be predicted is that within the category there will be an experience of sharedness, of similarity which is felt to be in marked contrast to the differentiating qualities of outsiders. When work relations are structured in this way, they carry a normative component: that is, people who associate share values, norms and knowledge. A central feature of this knowledge consists of the ways in which people 'like us' differ from the specified, targeted category of outsiders (for not everyone constitutes the outsiders with whom these comparisons of moral work are made: the outsider group are carefully defined and are necessary for the continuation of the insiders with their contrasted qualities).

One of the main features of this body of values and knowledge is that they support each other in that because of what is known to be characteristic of the target outsiders, certain forms of behaviour become necessary and consequently, virtuous. Thus it is wrong for junior policemen to inform on their colleagues to senior officers because everyone knows that the behaviour in question is normal and necessary, and that senior officers may act on the information they receive in order to protect themselves, or to advance their own careers. Their careerism is well known, as is their hypocrisy: the only sin is to be caught. Thus knowledge and necessary forms of sanctioned behaviour go hand in hand.

Frequently the knowledge in question stems not simply from work experience, but from extra-organisational sources. When relationship demarcations coincide with other axes of social differentiation, not only are the subsequent work patterns particularly marked, but extra-organizational knowledge and legitimations of these external demarcations will be employed internally, for example in the response of male workers to the introduction of female workers, where firmly grounded knowledge of women, their aspirations, emotionality, attitudes to work, priorities, physical capacity etc., are deployed to legitimate the demarcating of work relationships, and cross-gender attitudes and behaviour at work.

Finally, these phenomena are a source of identity — not of total identity, but of a contribution to identity. The significant work relationship demarcations are regarded, as we have seen, as articulating an important membership ('us') and an important difference ('us' from 'them'). In view of this it is only to be expected that such categories, being important, become important for our view of ourselves, in terms of the category label, and as exemplars of the virtues associated with the label. Thus in a case where a key differentiation is between us who are, say, men, and who display, necessarily, in our work various manly qualities, and where the targeted outsider category is women workers who, because of their gender, display various disabling (or unskilled, or work-cheapening, or dangerous) womanly qualities, it is to be expected that we will see ourselves at work and more widely, as among other things, manly, to a degree that another group of equally male workers who are not involved in such a combination of activities and qualities, would not.

In summary, the demarcation of relationships at work constitutes a highly important axis (or series of axes) of what are defined and experienced as highly salient, real, necessary and virtuous social differentiations. These patterns are as important for the way they fracture the work force, and for the consequent form of relations between demarcated categories, as for the form of solidaristic, identity-building, moralized relationships within the work-force. The former reprsents a basis of differentiation, rivalry, even opposition, which is sustained by the intimacy and culture and 'sameness' of each demarcated category. These structures of relationship need to be more fully described, and to be explained. Most of all we need to demonstrate their significance for work organizations' structure and functioning. Just how do these phenomena contribute to what happens within organizations? The following chapters will address this question through a consideration of two case studies.

2

Work relations and group solidarity: the London Fire Brigade

To reiterate the focus of this book and this chapter: at work, relationships among and between employees are patterned in certain definite, distinctive and significant ways. The significance of these structures of relationships lies in their meanings for those involved, and in their role as determinants of organizational functioning and process. This latter point, although firmly related to the former, is the key one, particularly since these structures are usually not patterned simply in response to formal requirements, and frequently constitute a basis for opposition to, or some freedom from, such requirements. In this chapter, two examples of such structuring, their origins and consequences, will be discussed. Our objective is to demonstrate the explanatory importance of employees' patterns of interaction for understanding events within the organizations in question. In each case a particular issue or perceived 'problem' is presented as requiring explanation.

As noted in the Preface, we shall consider two cases: the London Fire Brigade and the Indian Coal sector. We start, in this chapter, with the Fire Brigade.

Although originally formed in 1833 as the 'London Fire Engine Establishment', employing eighty full-time firemen in nineteen fire stations around the capital, the current London Fire Brigade (LFB) was formed in 1965 with the formation of the Greater London Council (GLC). Members of the LFB are employees of the GLC. The main objectives of the LFB are fire prevention and fire fighting, plus 'special services', (floods and other disasters). In 1982 the LFB answered 113,727 emergency calls.

The Brigade is organized on a divisional basis, with eleven divisions, comprising 114 fire stations and 7,638 staff of whom 6,800 are uniformed, and over 500 appliances. At the fire stations, work is divided between four watches, of approximately 12 firefighters, led by a station officer. The watch also includes sub-officers and leading firemen. Each watch works for a total of 42 hours per week, organized into two 9-hour day duties followed by two 15-hour night duties, followed by four days off duty.

Managerially, the watch is led by the station officer who works at and from the fire station, and works the same shifts as the watch. Recently a new post has been formed: Station Commander, of whom there is one per station. Above this, management is conducted from Divisional Headquarters or, ultimately, from Brigade Headquarters. Although, under special circumstances senior (i.e. Divisional Officer level) management can become involved in particularly big fires, for practical purposes, day-to-day management rests with the station officers, for not only are they with their watch for the duration of the work period, but senior management are located elsewhere and work different hours, and are largely concerned with adminstration.

A striking feature of the Brigade is that all members of the service start as firefighters. There is a single point of entry to the organization. Recruits start with a period of 14 weeks intensive training, and are then posted, on probation, to their first station. Promotion is on merit, assessed through annual appraisals and reports and by passing promotion examinations.

Despite the fact that the LFB has a single point of entry, and that promotion is by merit and examination, at the time of the installation of the new, Labour administration of the GLC in 1981, it was clear that only a very small proportion of firefighters were from non-white groups. Indeed the Chairman of the Public Services and Fire Brigade Committee, argued that although approximately one-seventh of London's population belonged to non-white ethnic minorities, and that the LFB had approximately 7,000 firemen, there were only seven black firemen in 1981. In fact even prior to the arrival of the Labour administration things were beginning to move. Previously recruitment was carried out through receiving unsolicited applications, but after 1980, vacancies were explicitly advertised in an effort to inform all sections of the community that vacancies were available and to widen the range of applicants. Later the system was changed more radically, and unsolicited applications were declared unacceptable: all had to be in response to an identified advertisement. At the same time in 1980 changes were made in the selection interview. Only one uniformed officer was now involved in each interview, and these selecting officers were carefully chosen, and trained. Later the system was changed back to two interviewers, but this time one was to be non-uniformed, from the Brigade's personnel department. The new administration was installed in May 1981. By December of the same year in Equal Opportunities policy was agreed, which stressed that the GLC is an Equal Opportunities employer: 'The aim of its policy is to ensure that no job application or employee receives less favourable treatment on the grounds of sex, race, colour, nationality, ethnic or national origins, marital status, sexual orientation, age, trade union activity, political or religious belief' (GLC, 1983).

The GLC Equal Opportunities policy was of course based upon, but went further than, Government Equal Opportunities legislation, notably the Race Relations Act, 1976, and the Sex Discrimination Act, 1975. Both these Acts made it unlawful to discriminate, directly or indirectly, on the basis of sex or race. But the Council's policy went further. If the law was, essentially, reactive (to identified breaches) and negative (in that they outlawed discrimination but did not suggest ways in which the objectives of the acts — fairness — could be achieved). Council policy actively sought to achieve the objective of the acts, through various means: internal and external.

Internal measures involved seeking to discover how fair the organization was, i.e. monitoring applications and success rates (from 1983); reviewing selection systems, procedures and standards and revising and training when necessary; initiating a programme of training courses for middle management (station officers and Divisional Officers) informing them of the law and policy and their responsibilities for Equal Opportunities. External measures involved carefully targeted recruitment advertising (ethnic press, for example), 'outreach' visits to youth clubs, schools and other centres, advertising material figuring black or female firefighters, plus, recently, pre-selection courses for those who had marginally failed the selection, and who were from disadvantaged and under-represented categories. The objective of these positive action initiatives was explicitly to encourage, inform (and, in some cases) to prepare an appropriate quality and quantity of applications from members of categories of people under-represented in the Brigade. To this end, such initiatives were accompanied by the formulation of annual target figures of recruitment from women and non-whites, in order to achieve a workforce which broadly reflected the ethnic, if not the sexual make-up of the London area. In fact, in 1985 these targets were 30 per cent for non-white ethnic categories and 3 per cent for women firefighters, these percentages being of recruits, and being targets, i.e. figures to aim at, but not necessarily to achieve. In fact as we shall see, actual percentages of ethnic and female recruits fell far short of these figures. The 3 per cent women figure is based on the United States experience. The report quoted research which argued that, in view of the types of task involved in firefighting, and types of physical attributes required to perform these tasks, and the implications of these for weight, size, height, fat to lean weight, and other indices, probably no more than 5 per cent of women would be physically capable to the work. Clearly, in this case, the likelihood of having many women in the fire service is very small.

The report of the GLC/LFB study tour of United States fire brigades, (1982) suggests that even a steady state figure of 8 per cent would be remarkable, and only achieved with rigorous pre-selection training. But the issue of having women in the LFB is not a numerical issue: most firemen will never work with a woman firefighter, even if the ambitious targets of the GLC are achieved. The 'problem' for firemen is something different: a matter of meaning, of pride, and of identity.

Initially, law and policy only applied to racial discrimination, for the LFB applied to the Home office for exemption from the provisions of the Sex Discrimination Act. Final rejection of this application occurred in late 1979. From 1980 the LFB was legally required to comply with both acts.

It was early appreciated that the implementation of these Acts and the GLC policy within the LFB was likely to be particularly problematic. The chair of the Fire Brigade committee wrote, in his introduction to the sensible and thorough report on the study tour of United States Fire departments, 'the new Labour Administration had to crack the recruitment policies and attitudes of the Brigade. We . . . formulated our plans on the basis that the Brigade, being a uniformed and disciplined civilian service, would be a tough nut to break. Certainly we expected it to be the toughest nut across the board of GLC departments' GLC, 20th July, 1982, p. 5). It was, and the recruitment and deployment of women firefighters was even tougher.

So far so good: there is nothing here that requires explanation. What we see is an organization with certain unusual structural features (the watch system; the separation of the watches, and watch management, from middle and senior management, socially, physically, geographically and temporally; the single point of entry; the danger of the work; and the social isolation the watch system, and the work itself could generate). This organization, was, prior to the Equal Opportunity Acts of 1976 and 1975, entirely unprepared even to consider the recruitment of female firefighters, and was probably loath to recruit non-whites. (It is necessary to be careful here because while the attitudes of LFB selectors and firemen towards the recruitment of non-whites were certainly important in seriously restricting the influx of such recruits, it is also probably true that, over time, the perceived closeness of the Brigade would deter many of these applicants from even trying: everybody 'knew' that the jobs were restricted to whites). And we must remember that a few non-whites — extremely few — did make it. All this needs no explanation; the attitudes towards the recruitment of non-whites were probably almost 'normal' in the early nineteen-seventies (which is a major reason why Equal Opportunity legislation was necessary), particularly for uniformed, disciplined organizations, where the jobs carried certain definite attractions, and where recruitment was largely 'endogamous' — from within the social group, consisting of those men known to, related to, neighbours of, or generally similar to in work background (merchant marine or services) serving firemen. It was a closed work, and as such it worked — at least for those within it.

But there is something that does need to be explained, and which is defined by many of the parties involved as a problem to be theorized over. This the nature, and the origins, of firemen's responses to the Equal Opportunities policy and programme. First we shall consider evidence about the nature of these reactions, then we shall try to account for these. Evidence on firemen's reactions was gathered from two sources: recruitment figures, and material gathered during lengthy discussions with over two-thirds of the station officers, during which they were extremely open and vociferous about their views on the Equal Opportunities policy and legislation.

Let us consider the recruitment figures for 1983. This was the year when training sessions for station officers and divisional officers began, and when discussions were held on Equal Opportunities issues with instructors at the LFB Training Centre, Southwark. This year too, saw advertising directed explicitly at non-whites and women, and the beginning of outreach work. 1983 was the year when the LFB publicly began to try to recruit women. Table 1 shows the numbers of applicants to the LFB in 1983, classified

Table 1 — Numbers of applicants to the LFB in 1983

	ACB		AB		EW		Other/UC	
	M	F	M	F	M	F	M	F
No. of apps.	435	14	116	0	7,390	30	200	25
% of total	5.3	0.2	1.4	0	90	0.4	2.4	0.3
No. started	17	00	3	0	473	5	11	0

according to ethnic origins, according to the GLC classification scheme. ACB is Afro-Caribbean Black; AB is Asian Brown, EW is European White and UC is unclassified. The categories are self-adminstered.

A total of five women were recruited in 1983. In this year, if we regard all those who, for whatever reason, chose to classify themselves as 'other', or who did not classify themselves at all, as belonging to minority ethnic categories, then the grand total for this year of non-white applications is 790 or 9.6 per cent of the total. Women constituted 0.8 per cent of applicants.

These figures could hardly be taken to represent a massive change in recruitment patterns, at least numerically. They were certainly not so regarded by the Equal Opportunities unit of the GLC, who viewing them in the light of the Council's determination to see 'its workforce broadly reflecting the ethnic and sexual make-up of London', would certainly have felt that these figures represented an unacceptably low level of achievement, some responsibility for which must reside with the Brigade's recruitment policies, selection methods, and staff attitudes. Our second source of material of fireman's responses is derived from discussions with many station officers. Station officers were asked: what do you think the Equal Opportunities law and policy are intended to achieve? What do you think they are achieving?

Responses to these questions were overwhelmingly negative, although not unanimously so. One unusual officer remarked that he thought the law and policy were intended to eradicate two of the greatest evils of our time: racism and sexism. But he turned out to be an Open University student! In terms of the elements of the firemen's culture, this was a highly deviant response.

Station officers' negative views of the Equal Opportunities (EO) programme had a number of related elements.

(1) When faced with the suggestion that EO law and policy were intended to achieve fairness — treating people in terms of their abilities and merits, and work-relevant characteristics rather than in terms of their sex or their race — the vast majority approved in principle. They were asked: if a woman joined the Brigade who was in every way suitable for and capable of doing, the work (in strength, attitudes, mechanical aptitudes, etc.) do you think she should be accepted? Typical responses to this question were to deny the possibility of such an occurrence because of the 'known' qualities of women, or more frequently, the 'known' deficiencies of the Brigade's selection system. In short, answers sought to avoid the uncomfortable and obvious issue of principle and to attack the likelihood in practice of the Brigade selecting suitable women. Clearly such a belief was highly functional: officers had to be able to convince themselves that women in the Brigade were not able to do the work. If there were women in the Brigade, then this could only be done by insisting that selection standards and procedures were flawed. However, officers would often insist that in principle they were not opposed to the recruitment of women. Some demurred, however, and would argue that mere formal qualification — even if achieved — was not sufficient to gain a woman entry. They should be rejected because of the damage they could do to the integration of the all-male watch, members of which ate, lived and slept together, as well as

worked together. But even those who agreed with the principle of fairness so qualified the conditions under which this principle could be exercised that it emerged as relatively useless and irrelevant. In fact the claimed commitment to fairness was used counter-productively in many cases to argue that having made such a commitment, the officer was consequently immune to criticism or accusations of bias or prejudice regardless of how outrageous his comments. It was also used to attack the EO programme itself which was frequently argued as being itself unfair because of the idiosyncratic manner in which practical fairness within the Brigade was defined. It was defined in terms of doing nothing to disturb existing patterns of power and access. Fairness was seen to reside in the natural order of things; active, purposeful interventions which in fact merely attempted to *correct* existing structures of inequality and unfairness were seen to be unfair to the degree that they were successful in redressing the balanced. Fairness was seen as demonstrated in the degree to which individuals were left free to treat people as they wished.

(2) The EO programme was, in consequence, argued as being in itself a case of positive discrimination in favour of under-represented groups. There were two aspects to this. First, although the distinction between positive action and positive discrimination was forcibly explained, officers insisted that in practice, within the Brigade, a policy of positive discrimination was occurring. Any initiative which was clearly (and justifiably) intended to redress some of the existing and historical imbalances of knowledge, attitude, confidence, qualification within the population of the London area, was seen as unfair to the extent that it addressed one section rather than another. The existing inequity in, for example, the distribution of knowledge about and enthusiasm for, joining the Brigade, as evident in the application figures, was seen not as representing an inherently unfair situation, but a normal, natural one which the policy was unfairly disturbing. Fairness could only be achieved through measures which affected all sections of the population equally and thus in effect, reflected the very pattern of discrimination and disadvantage which occasioned the EO legislation and which it was intended to eliminate. Secondly, it was argued that the implementation of EO policy and law within the Brigade was sectional, an example of positive discrimination in that what the GLC claimed were target recruitment figues, attempts to encourage and focus the Brigade's recruitment strategies and to assist the Brigade to achieve a more equitable representation of all ehtnic and sexual categories, were in fact quotas. They were claimed to impose pressure on senior officers, selectors, trainers, station officers, to force them to drop standards in order to achieve politically motivated recruitment figures. Two arguments were used to support these convictions. First, the 'obvious' and well known

decline in standards of recruits with respect to non-whites and women. Secondly, the equally well 'known' lack of integrity of senior management. Officers were asked, if they were so convinced that colleagues were prepared to allow standards to drop, whether they personally would also be prepared to deviate from accepted standards. Of course they insisted that they would not, while at the same time insisting that because of their careerism and opportunism, senior officers would have no such scruples.

(3) The officers were convinced that women firefighters were not able properly to do the work of firefighting. They were highly resistant to arguments on this point. Even if, in a discussion group, there was a station officer who was currently acting as an officer of a watch with a woman in it, and this officer was prepared to admit that she was in fact competent — as certainly happened — this information would be ignored by the rest of the group or defined as exceptional. A characteristic response to such evidence was to continue to question the officer about the woman's performance on various difficult or strenuous operations until finally he admitted some area of weakness. This was then triumphantly seized upon and identified as the evidence they had all expected. The capacity of the officers to select evidence to support their convictions, and to ignore contrary evidence was highly developed. In fact the station officers had it nicely both ways. If a woman or a non-white clearly and publicly failed, at selection or training or probation, this was taken as evidence of the innate inability of that class of recruit to do firefighting work. If on the other hand they did not fail, this was taken as evidence of senior management's opportunistic manipulation of standards. Firemen *know* that women cannot — and should not — be firefighters. For some this was because of physical strength; for some it was because of their innate femininity (particularly their well known tendency to become victims of their hormones prior to, during and after menstruation); for others it was their sexuality which would grossly disturb the male members of the watch. All of these views were conveniently supported by anecdote which circulated within the incredibly vigorous station rumour network.

(4) For others of a more sophisticated bent, women were not in principle necessarily poor firefighters, but the actual women currently in the Brigade were not, as everyone knew, competent. How then were they selected in the first place? Because of informal positive discrimination. So two birds could be felled with one argument: women were defined as incompetent; it attributed their being in the Brigade to an unfair policy (thus undermining it), and attributed this to an, unprincipled, opportunistic senior management (thus maligning them and labelling their reassurances about the EO policy and the quality of the women recruits as inherently untrustworthy).

(5) Finally we must mention the vigour of station officers' attitudes towards the EO policy. This was probably the most striking feature of their reactions: they were angry, sometimes to the point of incoherence, often to the point of obscenity. Their anger and distress were real. Frequently officers insisted that their pride and confidence in their work was destroyed, that they personally were diminished.

Station officers' responses revealed a powerful and important clustering of views, knowledge and beliefs. They were highly resistant to the programme, and saw it largely and probably almost entirely in negative terms as an example of institutionalized unfairness, foisted on them by a management prepared to sacrifice standards and traditions and loyalties in order cynically to keep in with a highly politicized GLC administration. This response revolved around a conviction of their own essential fairness and reasonableness, of the irrelevance of the EO programme, of the 'well-known' failings of the women firefighters, of the dishonesty of senior officers' statements about, and commitment to, the EO programme, and of the likelihood that this programme would generate the very attitudes and behaviour it was intended to eliminate. This is an ingenious cluster of arguments. It leaves the station officers safely beyond accusations of prejudice, thus legitimating their opinions (I'm no racist, but . . .) while attributing any discrimination either to the EO policy itself, or to the consequences of the programme.

These ideas need to be explained. Clearly, Braverman and post-Braverman theories have nothing to say on these issues, since they have nothing to do with work design, or with class forces or class consequences. Nevertheless they are of importance, to those who may fall victim to these ideas (non-whites or women) or to those who wish to achieve fairness in employing organizations, or to those who wish to be able to explain the structure and dynamics of large organizations.

There are two theories of these responses of fireman which are highly pervasive and available, not least to the protagonists of the struggle around the installation of the EO programme. One argues the racism and sexism of firemen; the other the institutionalization of racism and sexism within the Brigade culture. Both have a germ of truth, but both are wrong.

The first is untenable because it is reductionist, simplistic and circular. Of course some firemen are racist and sexist. But to explain the large-scale resistance and bitterness described above in terms of individual's attitudes is to put the cart before the horse: individual's attitudes are products of their membership of the community of firemen, not causes of the Brigade's distinctive culture. There is something about the situation of firemen and their officers which makes it particularly likely that they will resist programmes like the EO programme.

Similarly, to argue that firemen's organizational culture is somehow essentially chauvinist is also to miss a step in the explanation. We are told that their culture is chauvinist because firemen resist the EO programme, and that they resist this programme because they are members of a chauvinist culture. It is true that certain attitudes and behaviour, negative or unfriendly towards non-whites and women are inherent in the culture, but a satisfactory explanation seeks to explain *why* firemen's culture is chauvinist, rather than simply to assert that it is.

How then can we explain this resistance to the GLC/LFB EO policy?

First, we must assert its social, collective character. Obviously in the discussion points were made by *individuals,* sometimes by a number of individuals. Nevertheless it is possible to describe these as social because of the way in which such utterances could be seen to be articulations of a shared view. There are a number of elements to this: first, there was the sheer pervasiveness of the point of view described earlier; it was certainly the majority point of view. But this is not to say that by any means *all* station officers subscribed to it, for some certainly did not. A number dissented; many indicated their distance from this point of view by their silence, others quietly signalled their disapproval during break periods. The social nature of the responses does not depend on their pervasiveness merely: it is also indicated by the *moral* nature of this point of view: officers who articulated these attitudes were applauded (which encouraged them further) officers who publicly dissented were greeted with silence, or with heavily ironic banter. Further, the rumour and gossip systems were active to legitimate the acceptable points of view, to confirm their good sense and accuracy.

From this it seems that we have a social phenomenon to explain: not just simply a collection of individual points of view. How can this be explained in terms of the patterning of social relationships within the brigade? We shall focus on three issues: the isolation of the watch from other sections of the management hierarchy; the extent of trust between these two sections of management and how distrust is structurally determined; and socially structured bases of resistance to EO programmes in terms of the patterned interests of firemen and station officers.

These three issues translate into two major concerns of station officers: the historical, closed selection system, prior to the EO programme plus the particular forms of vocational pride available to firemen and fire officers, incorporating, as this work identity does, the notion of public service and manliness; and the consequences of the single point of entry for relationships between tiers of management, particularly across the major break, already described, between station and division, plus the managerial isolation of the watch from other levels of managment. We shall address these in turn.

JOBS FOR THE BOYS AND PRIDE IN THE JOB

Prior to the EO initiative of the 1981 labour administration, (anticipated to some extent by the previous administration), the LFB was largely filled from a particular social segment of the population of London. An index of this can be gauged from the fact that even as late as mid-1985, over 70 per cent of applicants did not respond to particular job advertisements, but simply applied for jobs on the basis of their knowledge of the Brigade and the job, knowledge that was available within a relatively limited social area of London. It is safe to assume that this reflected candidates' membership of those communities within which access to Brigade jobs was known to be reasonably secure. Of course, any particular (white, male) individual, applying to join the Brigade could not be sure that he would achieve a place. Selection was always a major hurdle. In the 1980s, well over 90 per cent of applicants would be rejected. The LFB was always, and quite properly, a highly discriminating employer.

But the question is, among whom was it discriminating? How widespread was the LFB search for suitable candidates? The answer must be that at least prior to the EO initiative, the Brigade was prepared to rely on informal recruitment advertising, within the community represented by those who were already members. A large, but unknown, number of candidates and successful recruits were related to, were friends or neighbours of, or were generally in backgrounds similar to, serving officers. Thus was access to the occupation effectively closed: in order to have a real chance of entry it was necessary to be a member of the community that constituted the labour market for the Brigade; however, and this is critical, membership of this community did not, in itself by any means guarantee membership of the Brigade. To be from the same background milieu as the serving firemen, and to be socially connected to serving firemen was a necessary but not a sufficient social basis for entry to the occupation. It was also necessary to pass the demanding selection tests.

The combination of these two factors: limited accessibility, allied to high competitiveness within a delimited pool, had a number of definite consequences. First, firemen, and fire officers, were remarkably homogeneous in social origins, previous occupational experience, social attitudes, and general social characteristics and culture, i.e. white, working class, often with a services background, or some experience of a disciplined regime, etc. This homogeneity encouraged a much higher level of shared occupational culture than would otherwise have been possible — see below. It also meant that this culture was more meaningful because of the way it could reflect, and resonate with, shared out-of-work experience and attitudes, particularly with respect to attitudes to blacks and women. But the competitiveness within the original starting group, which resulted in most cases in one candidate in twenty actually being accepted for training, meant that successful candidates regarded their success as evidence of their particular, individual worth. Consequently they were likely to regard their occupational role as a source of considerable pride and achievement, to incorporate it as a major element of their identity. This did not mean only that they saw themselves as firemen, or officers, although they certainly did. It also, and crucially, meant that they were likely to assimilate what they learnt to regard as the necessary skills or traits demanded by successful execution of the work into their self-images. Particularly important among these assimilated traits were the characteristics which they saw as essentially masculine, or manly. For us in this book to describe how station officers saw the qualities required by the work in these terms should not be interpreted as implying that the author does not see fighting fires, rushing into burning buildings, scaling the outside of burning buildings which might collapse imminently, as not courageous. Far from it. What is at issue here however is not the bravery involved in firefighting, or the public service, but the fireman's conviction that these qualities are somehow more likely to reside in men than in women.

The firemen and the officers had no doubts at all that fighting fires was manly work, done by men, requiring manly attributes of strength, bravery, discipline, emotional control, manly camaraderie. Not only was firefighting manly, and done exclusively by men, it was also only possible in a social situation of men working and living together cosily and amicably in the *social* situation of the all-male watch (strangely this was often described as 'family-like', which not only glossed over the common pathologies of family life — conflict, violence, emotionality, all of which were very evident on the watch — but it also ignored the essential difference between families and watches: that the former were composed of members of both sexes).

This watch camaradie, was claimed by officers to be necessary in order to develop the necessary team building required for firefighting discipline and interdependence. Frequently officers would point out that when a pair of firefighters entered a burning building, unable to see because of smoke, wearing heavy breathing apparatus, feeling their way up stairs which may already have partially collapsed, in a space which could, at any moment suddenly and possibly fatally either ignite, or collapse, the necessary dependence of one firefighter on another was a great deal more — and more significant — than the dependence of a factory worker on his/her neighbour on the line. Such mutual dependence and confidence, it was argued, could only be generated in an all-male environment. Women would fatally disturb the intimacy of the all-male group by introducing an unforgivable degree of strangeness. More than this they would introduce sex, and thus potentially divide firemen from firemen because of their high developed sexuality.

We can see from this that to the officers — and the firemen they represented — the introduction of women to the watch was seen as a threat to tradition in a number of ways. First the EO programme in general represented a definite and explicit counter to traditional forms of recruitment which were not only convenient to firemen in that they ensured a supply of like-minded recruits, they also served continuously to confirm the measure of their achievement in gaining access to the brigade.

Secondly, such programmes undermined officers' senses of achievement in their occupational careers and identities. Since the EO programme explicitly set out to encourage and inform, and to some degree, through pre-selection training, to prepare recruits for the selection system, this was seen to devalue the achievement of those who had made it without such assistance. It was not therefore surprising that officers constantly likened the EO programme to the recruitment drive of 1974, where, because of an increase in the number of shifts worked, the LFB had to increase its workforce by 25 per cent very rapidly and thus, by many accounts, was prepared to drop standards. So, at least it was claimed, ten years later, with great bitterness among those who saw their achievement thus devalued, and who liked to hark back to the golden days of their selection when standards were really high. By evaluating standards of entry, station officers indirectly but deliberately evaluated standards of recruits, themselves included.

Thirdly, the modifications to traditional methods of recruitment were quite considerable: serving firemen were no longer allowed to give references; all applications had to be in response to a recruitment drive, station officers were no longer allowed to distribute application forms to interested potential candidates who came in off the street. These changes had the obvious and explicit intention of replacing an informal, implicit, closed, 'word of mouth' recruitment and selection system by a formal, open system. This was not only an attack on a system which was traditional and familiar to the officers, more importantly it was an attack on their control of recruitment and selection. Prior to the EO programme, station officers controlled both selection and recruitment to a considerable degree: they were the selectors, the interviewers, the testers, the officers who screened the application forms; they were also very frequently the referees of candidates; they were the people who first met the station visitor interested in learning more of the Brigade, and presumably played this gatekeeper role in a manner which reflected the preferences of the brigade culture. More than this, by allowing recruitment to occur by word of mouth within restricted sections of London (while within others, as later 'outreach' work was to show, the word was that there was no point in applying to the Brigade because as everyone knew, that was a white job) the overall pattern of perpetuation of the social and cultural composition of the Brigade was ensured.

All this was changed by the EO programme, and so station officers found that not only their control over recruitment and selection, but the very pattern and composition of recruitment was changing radically. In fact interestingly, because of its significance to station officers, the actual scale of the change was frequently grossly exaggerated by officers. Because the nature of the change mattered greatly *qualitatively,* the *quantity* of the change was frequently seen to be much greater than it was in fact. Actual recruitment figures such as those given in Table 1 invariably suprised station officers.

To summarize this section, we have suggested that one major reason for station officers' (and firemen's) resistance to the EO programme was the way in which changes in recruitment and selection practices, and the nature of recruits — particularly the introduction of women — clashed with station officers' self-images as firemen, and as representing manly work virtues, their sense of achievement in entering the occupation, and in mastering the work, their control of the recruitment and selection process, and their membership of a closed, familiar and all-male world which they largely controlled. But while these reactions may be understandable in terms of the radical changes represented by the EO programme, as far as the station officers are concerned, the situation, and station officers' grievances were greatly amplified by another set of factors which served to create a distance between divisional management and fire station, and it is to this issue that we now turn.

DIVISION AND SOLIDARITY

By virtue of two important features of the social structuring of relationships within the Brigade, station officers and the watches they command are systematically isolated from — indeed in some respects, almost opposed to — higher levels of management. This separation has very significant consequences for station officers' attitudes to the EO programmes. It represents a dramatic case of the basic thesis of this book: that the patterning of social relationships — however inadvertent and informal —

can play a major role in the determination of organizational process and activity.

The two key features have already been mentioned in passing: the social isolation of the station and the watch, and the social — indeed personal — consequences of the recruitment practice, and philosophy, of single point of entry.

Although large firefighting operations may occasion the deployment of more appliances, and more personnel, than are available to a single watch (which usually has two applicances available in the station), nevertheless the working unit remains the watch. For although this unit may be added to, and although sometimes, for big jobs, divisional management will be brought in to take command of multi-station emergencies, nevertheless, the watch is always the basic — and usually the sole — working unit. Whoever else they may sometimes work with, the watch usually work together. Members of a watch also live together during the four phases of the shift. There are good grounds for maintaining that when a group of socially and, until recently, sexually homogeneous people live together over long periods they will develop stronger and more intense bonds than would develop among people who have more fleeting contacts. If we add to this that these members of the watch are also sharing danger, hardship, and excitement, then the possibilities of a highly intense social grouping developing are very strong. This is not to say that such groupings always developed; there were accounts of pathological watches, where things went very wrong indeed. The watch need not — indeed probably usually does not — generate bonds of affection among *all* the members. But it certainly develops bonds of high intensity, even if they are sometimes of irritation, even hostitility. And whatever happens, the watch remains the key membership group.

This intensity of relationships within the watch (including the station officer who, although the senior member of the watch, is still unquestionably a member of the watch) is important enough as a basis of watch solidarity, but it is greatly amplified by virtue of the separation of the watch from other watches in the same station, and to an even greater degree, its separation from other levels of management. As noted earlier this separation is *temporal* (the time of work), *physical* (*where* the watch and divisional management work) and *organizational* (the sort of work they do, and the connections between them). What we find then is that virtue of the team-building features of the watch experience and work, allied to the separating factors that divide the watch from other levels of management, the watch tends to be as close internally and horizontally as it is estranged externally and vertically.

Because station officers represent the first, major line of management, and because they work more closely with the watch than with superior levels of management (from whom, as we have seen, they are isolated), station officers find themselves isolated managerially from senior management, whom they regard not as a source of support, but as a source of sanctions. Their closeness to the watch makes it difficult to enforce discipline, and tempting to allow the rules to be bent or even ignored, particularly such rules which impinge on station social life. Station officers are also loath to rely on formal sanctions and prefer to handle issues of their authority through force of personality rather than rely on their formal authority. To 'go by the book' is probably regarded by station officers and members of the watch alike, as a sign of weakness, at least if relied on too frequently. It is an obvious and predictable feature of relations between the station officer and the watch that the officer would be prepared to condone a degree of deviation from the 'book' (at least on regulations which were widely regarded as inessential, or unrealistic) in order to achieve a degree of consent and everyday give and take. After all the station officer is not only isolated from senior levels of management; he is also, potentially isolated from his station officer colleague. He is alone with his watch, and it is essential that this working unit gets on well, and works well, and lives well, together. This can probably only be achieved if the officer is prepared — to some degree — to trade formal, ritualistic enforcement of each and every regulation, for a measure of goodwill, if only to demonstrate that his authority does not depend solely on his rank. This means that managerially, the station officer is probably as loyal, and as close, to his watch as to the chain of command. This does not affect behaviour on the fireground, where entirely professional criteria and decision making is paramount; but it probably does affect ordinary, everyday life at the station.

Not only is the station officer close, managerially, to the watch; he is at the same time, managerially estranged from senior management. Again this does not apply to actual firefighting, where sheer professionalism, and the force of the chain of command and established procedures are dominant. But in general man-management terms, the station officers felt that they frequently lacked the support of senior officers. If, for example, they wished to impose their formal authority within the watch, many officers mentioned that they had found that their senior officer would not automatically support them. Also, it was frequently suggested that senior management's response to station officers' requests for advice was consistently: 'if you don't know how to do the job I'll find someone who can'. Station officers thus claimed to find themselves caught between two conflicting tensions: if they tried to impose their formal authority *vis-à-vis* the watch they might well find themselves without formal support from senior divisional management, and thus they would publicly lose prestige in the eyes of the watch; on the other hand if they asked the advice of senior management before taking action they might well find themselves losing credibility in the eyes of senior management.

It can be appreciated how these tensions would serve to exacerbate the likelihood of station officers defining their interests in terms not of formal, hierarchical management, but of the wellbeing off the watch. Policy, particularly on contentious issues, like the EO programme, could be sacrificed to the watch's opposition, in order to maintain watch solidarity. Station officers' formal authority, which could only rarely be used (outside of the fireground) was, it was felt, devalued by lack of support on discipline issues; their informal authority, on the other hand, which was very important, functionally, was dependent on their achieving close links with the watch, and complying with watch culture and morality. Clearly this situation would tend to amplify the processes of internal, watch solidarity, and external estrangement already described. it would also have definite consequences for the nature and direction of officers' sympathies and trust, and therefore for their willingness to believe, and to accept the sense of senior management policy in contentious areas, as, for example the EO programme. But these difficulties are greatly exacerbated by another feature of brigade life: station officers' attitudes towards their seniors in general.

It is a strange and delightful truism of sociology that people's experience of a situation can sometimes have very little to do with its objective nature. We have seen a small example of this already. Because the change in recruitment and selection methods and procedures represented a serious and unwelcome reduction in station officers' control over the recruitment process, they tended grossly to overestimate the statistical change brought about by the change in policy. Station officers' experience of career development within the brigade demonstrates a similar and equally important feature. We have noted that the brigade has a single point of entry and that promotion is organized on highly formalized grounds: established minimum periods of incumbency of various positions prior to promotion, the requirement of various internal examinations and courses, and formalized probationary, and appraisal procedures. As far as possible the promotion system is formalized, open and routinized. However, station officers indicated, indirectly, profound dissatisfaction with their promotion chances. This dissatisfaction took its most obvious form in the shape of a vigorous and pervasive cynicism concerning senior management.

A classic study in Industrial Sociology, *The American Soldier*, was the first to reveal a paradoxical feature of peoples' work attitudes which was evident also in the LFB: the greater the chance of promotion, the more dissatisfied people are with their promotion chances. Although this makes no objective sense, it makes a great deal of subjective sense to the people concerned. What occasions personal dissatisfaction with work conditions is not necessarily what they are objectively like, or how they objectively compare with those of unknown and unnoticed others, but how our progress compares with others like us: how we progress in comparison with others. If, as a station officer, we find that we have made career progress, this will probably be at the same time a source of pride (see the section above on work identity) which will stimulate the appetite for further progress; and a source of discontent in that we can see others — who are like us, being from the same background, and sharing many characteristics with us — who are doing better.

The fact that all firefighters start at the same position, and start from more or less the same background and qualification (very few have degrees, for example, and range of variation of formal qualification is slight) means that when some start to push ahead of the others, the ones left behind are faced with a major problem: how to explain to themselves — and their fellows and subordinates — their *relative* failure. The answer is simple: their successful colleagues' career achievements must be attributed not to their superior competence or work records (for that would be to accept public and conspicuous, relative inferiority) but to other, extrinisic, and, if possible, unfavourable factors. Ideally their success must be defined in terms of, and as a consequence of, their possession of *undersirable* qualities, and thus their very success can be publicly defined as evidence of moral failure. This is exactlyy what station officers do. Unable to explain their colleagues' success by reference to their superior, advantaged, privileged starting position; unable, unlike academics, to claim that their rivals' promotion was because they qualified on one of the various selection criteria which was essentially, ideally, peripheral to the *real* objectives of the job, station officers were forced to explain their colleagues' success by reference to their excessive concern to be promoted: i.e. their careerism, their opportunism, and their preparedness to please senior management, to 'kow-tow' to their whims, to sacrifice all other values for the sake of promotion. In this way those who broke solidarity with the watch by seeking — and achieving — promotion were punished (in their absence) by those who felt jealous, or, as they saw it, betrayed.

This interpretation may seem fanciful. But it was not glibly arrived at. Initially, the frequent disparaging stories about the integrity and competence or untrustworthiness of senior management were taken as worth attention, until it became apparent that what was interesting was not the content of the stories, but their very existence. They were treated as symptoms rather than as descriptions. Of course all those who see colleagues promoted over them are likely to suffer pangs of jealousy or resentment. But what characterizes the LFB it is argued, is that the structured homogeneity, and early solidarity of officers, allied to the very openness and formality of the selection systems and criteria, plus the consequences of the single point of entry, generate a need to develop a collective mythology — an organization fairy tale — which explains away what would otherwise be personally and collectively uncomfortable. Because so many people are in the same position, *vis-á-vis* those who achieve promotion, the solution becomes a collective one, and thus feeds upon itself. It becomes 'taken-for-granted', a fact of brigade life.

Now this has serious implications for the reactions of station officers and members of the watch to the EO programme. We have argued that the watch is both unusually close and solidaristic, and is isolated organizationally, temporally and geographically from senior levels of divisional management. We now find that this isolation is compounded by a distrust of senior management. When this situation is applied to officers' reactions to the EO programme we can identify the likely determinates of the level of resistance we described earlier. This programme is seen as essentially unfair, because of what are seen as senior management's preparedness to sacrifice standards in order to satisfy the targets of their GLC bosses. (This conviction was not dented by discussing the actual levels of recruitment which showed how the targets were not in fact being achieved: the conviction was inviolable, irrefutable.)

The conviction that women were unable in practice to do the job of firefighting (which was also inviolable) also derived from the combination of factors described above. Because of the necessary manliness of the work, it was obvious that no woman could do it (to accept that they could would be to force a reordering of officers' identities). Since women obviously could not do the work, for senior officers to support and enforce a policy of recruitment of women could only be explained in terms of their careerism and opportunism. Since women were, as all firemen knew, unable to fight fires, then if women were in fact recruited it was obvious that they must have been selected through the deliberate manipulation of standards (senior officers' opportunism again). When senior officers insisted that they had no interest in standards being dropped to allow inferior, female recruits to join the brigade, this was actually interpreted as being a direct instruction that more women were required, no matter what. When it came to analyses of women's performance as firefighters only one source of evidence was respected: other firemen. They of course 'knew' that women were failing, and were disturbing the previously all-male watches.

The recruitment of non-white men encountered opposition largely because of the disturbance to traditional, closed, systems of recruitment and selection, discussed earlier. No officer ever maintained that non-whites were less able than white. Opposition was more directed against the 'unfairness' of treating this category of potential recruit more favourably than whites. Fairness was seen to reside in the perpetuation of the status quo — with all its (natural) advantages for white firemen and officers. Station officers saw their own selection — against the odds — as fair, and as a fair reflection of their merits *vis-á-vis* the many unsuccessful candidates. They had achieved entry without any help. That was fairness — to let things be and to let individuals achieve their own destinies. The idea that whole categories of candidate might be systematically advantaged or disadvantaged was rejected, as was any form of intervention which attempted to correct or allow for, the privilege or disadvantage of categories of individuals.

We have come a long way from our starting point; but this description of recent events within the LFB is necessary and useful because it represents an example of the *heuristic* utility of our general approach. Station officers' resistance to the EO programme has been couched not in terms of their chauvinism, or their 'culture' of conservatism, but in terms of the ways in which their situation within their employing brigade allies them with some groups — the watch — and separates them from others — senior management — and the way in which recruitment patterns amplify the solidarity experience by a highly homogeneous workforce. In short, our analysis has been in terms of the systematic structuring of social relationships within the organization, and the role of such patterns for solidarity, estrangement, identity, homogeneity. We shall now continue our analysis with a consideration of a very different case: an Indian coal mine.

3

Work relations and group division: the Moonidih coal project

In August 1978 a power support face first started working at Moonidih mine, Bihar, India. This was an extremely important occasion. Although a degree of partial mechanization had existed earlier in Indian mines this was the first fully mechanized face. The Moonidih installation had been selected and set up as a pilot installation of the programme of modernization which had been initiated in an attempt to improve the output from Indian mines. It was most important that the first fully mechanized longwall face was a success. But it wasn't. To date it still is not working to anything like the expected output targets. The research discussed here is an attempt to contribute to an understanding of the reasons for this disappointment.

First some background to coal in India, to Coal India Ltd., and to the modernization programme of which the Moonidih initiative was a major part.

The most common coal-getting method, underground, in India is the traditional bord and pillar method. This method involves cutting coal from around a series of pillars which are left standing to support the roof. This is highly wasteful of coal. It is also an inefficient method of winning coal, for the degree to which coal cutting and coal removal can be mechanized under bord and pillar conditions, is limited. Within the bord and pillar mines, for example, mechanized coal-getting equipment was used. But altogether these machines probably account for something like 3 per cent of underground production. But not only is this total small, this partial use of machines cannot truly be described as mechanized coal getting — it is only sensible to talk of mechanized coal getting when machines are used in particular combinations which add greatly to the efficiency of the individual units. A mechanized longwall face involves three elements: first, the coal is cut across a long face, often 100 metres long, and no coal pillars are left.

Secondly, the coal is cut mechani-cally by a coal shearer — an electrically driven machine which traverses the face, cutting coal with a large drum on which is mounted a large number of picks. This shearer is accompanied by conveyor-belt coal transport systems, the most important of which, the Armoured Face Conveyor, travels under the shearer, collecting the coal as it is cut, and moves forward with the cutting machine as it advances after each traverse of the face. Thirdly, a roof-support system is required. As all the coal is cut right across the face, the roof is left unsupported. Mechanical support is therefore necessary. This is supplied by a series of hydraulic roof supports which advance along the length of the face, behind the shearer. As the shearer advances, the roof supports are lowered and push themselves forward hydraulically up to the newly positioned shearer. Once they no longer support the roof behind the shearer, it collapses safely.

There is no question that this method of coal getting is far more efficient and effective than the bord and pillar and unmechanized method. The output from a mechanized bord and pillar face is about a quarter of the output from a mechanized longwall face.

For twenty years, until the late nineteen-seventies, Indian mining engineers concentrated on the adoption of mechanized bord and pillar working. The results were not successful. By 1979, projected output from such systems totalled only 3 per cent of total underground production. In view of the urgent national requirement of increased coal output, for coal consitutes by far the most important source of energy (over one-third of the nation's energy needs, plus an important proportion of the needs of the industrial sector), it can be, and has been, argued that India's continuing industrial development depends on the increasing supply of coal. It was clear, by the middle nineteen-seventies, that a programme of moderniza-tion of the mines had to be initiated. For example, although output in the year ending 1982/83 was around 130 million tonnes, The Indian Depart-ment of Coal estimated that demand for coal in year ending 1984/5 would be more than 150 million tonnes, and by 1990, a staggering 230 million tonnes. Such quantities, and such rapid increase in level of output, could not possibly be achieved with traditional methods, or with traditional coal-getting technologies. What was clearly necessary was a vigorous commit-ment to the installation of fully mechanized power support longwall faces, for only this method and technology is capable of achieving the levels of output that were required by the National plans for the industry. As the chief mining engineer from the Central Mine Planning and Design Insti-tute, Ranchi, wrote: 'Mechanized longwall mining is the most dominant method of mining in the world in which the biggest technological break-throughs have been achieved in recent years. This system holds all records of production, productivity and safety in the world coal mining scene'. The

British National Coal Board team, which visited and studied CIL strategy and its modernization programme, in 1979, stated, as its 13th recommendation, that CIL should concentrate on the introduction of longwall mining in its fully mechanized form. This recommendation was accepted by Coal India Ltd (CIL).

In 1976, Coal India Ltd's planning and design institute produced a project report for self-advancing powered-support faces at Moonidih. Two years later the first powered-support face was introduced in 1978 in Moonidih, with UK coal sector grant aid.

Moonidih colliery is within the Jharia coalfield, 260 km north-west of Calcutta. Moonidih comes under the control of Bharat Coking Coal Ltd. The colliery at Moonidih was designed in collaboration with Kopex, a Polish company, in the 1960s. The colliery is at the centre of the attempt to modernize the Indian coal industry. From a British point of view, as NCB engineers and mine planners commented, the mine is remarkably rich in good quality accessible deposits lying in rich thick seams (ranging in thickness from 1.0 to 3.0 metres).

At the time of writing, late 1985, there are three powered-support systems at Moonidih: the elderly Kopex system which is currently on the surface being overhauled, and two Anderson Strathclyde/Dowty systems. The second of these is very new and on the occasion of the author's recent visit — late 1985 — had not yet started production. But this was imminent.

Powered-support faces work on 'panels' — enormous square areas of coal — bounded on three sides by 'roads', one of which is a main road which may have numerous panels off it. The other two roads constitute the two boundaries of the panel. At the top of the square or panel, is the face, where the shearer works across the whole breadth of the face of the panel. The shearer then slowly retreats until it is once more alongside the main road. It is normal for the distance from the starting face to the main base road to be about 1 kilometre. The shearer travels at about 1 kilometre a year. The two side roads are used for access by men and machines to the face, and for the conveying of cut coal. Since August 1978, when the first powered-support face started work, four complete panels have been extracted by British supplied equipment, and since it is the contribution of these machines on which we have data, our attention will be largely restricted to them.

THE PERFORMANCE OF POWERED SUPPORT SYSTEMS AT MOONIDIH

The output from the mechanized powered-support faces was disappointing, by all accounts. Everyone agreed on this. But they disagreed radically on the causes of the disappointment. British Mining Consultants, a British-based mining consultancy organization that offered professional consultancy throughout all stages of the modernization programme, and whose officers played a major part in attempting to identify and redress difficulties, argued that production results from the first three panels were as follows:

1st panel: 13 months production, average tonnes per day 606
2nd panel: 12 months production, average tonnes per day 734
3rd panel: 10 months production, average tonnes per day 518

These output figures must be seen in the context of target output figures. Writing in late 1983, BMC consultants noted that in the 35 months of actual production, average daily production was 597 tonnes. The target figure was nearly 1,500 tonnes per day. An expert group made up of CIL and Department of Coal officers, set up in late 1983, argued that output against targets in the four panels then completed at Moonidih were as follows:

Target TPD	Face	Av. TPD	% achieved
1000	PS–1	606	60.6
1000	PS–2	734	73.4
1000	PS–3	518	51.8
1350	PS–4	880	65.0

There is not doubt that these figures were more than merely disappointing. They were widely taken to be indications of a serious problem. As noted, Moonidih was at the front of the drive to modernize the Indian coal industry. It was a modern mine, although many features required modification in the light of the mechanization process, as we shall see. The machinery had been carefully chosen and installed. It was essential that the Indian coal sector be modernized if yields were to be increased in line with known and projected demand. The technology installed was known to work elsewhere; it was the best system — the only modern system — yet it was not working well. The problem rapidly became a public, and a national, even international one. A report in the *Financial Times* of 11 June 1984 says of the modernization programme: 'Concern about under-performance of equipment both foreign and domestic, say officials, is threatening to undermine the industry's $1.3bn a year investment programme. So far, India's switch to mechanized underground coal mining has been as maddeningly slow as its ability to bring new mining projects on stream'. In the same report the new chairman of CIL was quoted as insisting that: 'I have given a blunt order that we will not buy a piece of equipment, not even a chisel, without a performance guarantee — a financially binding guarantee.'

The chairmans forceful comments indicate both the level of concern at the results from Moonidih, and the most prevalent form of explanation among CIL officers (and, indeed, Department of Coal officers): that the technology used was somehow at fault. Because explanation of problems can play an important role in the persistence and definition of the problem, it is interesting briefly to consider some of the major explanations on offer for what was generally agreed to be a serious problem.

EXPLANATIONS OF POOR LEVELS OF OUTPUT FROM POWERED-SUPPORT FACES AT MOONIDIH

A marked difference in explanation was apparent between those offered by CIL and the Department of Coal, on the one hand, and British Mining Consultants and British manufacturers on the other. This split was in itself important, as well shall see.

British Mining Consultants (BMC) explained the results in terms of two main types of factors: geological and human/system. For example, the report of March 1983 on the progress of mechanized faces at Moonidih to that date assessed the results of the faces, accepted that they had consistently failed to achieve the targeted production levels, and attributed these results to four factors:

> geological faults in all the three panels
> deficiencies in the coal clearance system
> staff inexperience
> poor machine maintenance

Discussions with BMC consultants, with Moonidih management, and with other informed observers suggested that all four factors were important. However, many Indian observers argued that this analysis was partial, that it avoided the central issue: the machinery itself. The same report quoted above, mentions early on that when the BMC team first arrived at Moonidih to discuss the poor performance of the mechanized faces, local management offered the following factors in explanation:

> geological faults;
> damage done to the armoured face conveyor, plus interior quality
> local supplied spares
> the shearer 'tripping out' due to overload
> shortage of spares for the powered supports and the face lighting

The BMC report exhaustively analyses what was going wrong, but attributes the numerous cases of damage to the machinery in terms of misuse or abuse of the system, by geological circumstance or direct human agency, or poor maintenance. Their report lists numerous cases of bad practice, and describes the efforts of 'guidance, persuasion and encouragement' expended to instil support for a new mining system.

In December of the same year in another assessment, BMC consultants again stressed the role of six key factors:

coal clearance problems
inadequate supplies of spare parts to hand
maintenance problems
lack of sufficient quantity of experienced personnel, plus too rapid promotion of trained staff
lack of effective incentive scheme for face-workers.

From this informed and thorough survey we can see that, at least for BMC consultants, the problem was caused by a combination of geological, human, system and infrastructural factors. But what of Moonidih management, CIL, and Department of Coal officers? Their explanations have already been indicated in the remarks of the chairman of CIL quoted earlier: the problem is the technology. Hence the need for 'performance guarantees'. Indian analysts would not dispute *all* the elements of the BMC/ manufacturers explanation, particularly those that refer to machine damage, and geological conditions. But they would insist that the problem lies deeper — in the essential inappropriateness of the systems installed at Moonidih. What Anderson Strathclyde, or BMC see as human or system problems (knowledge, attitude, motivation, training, etc.), the Indian commentators tended to define as machine deficiencies. Somehow, for some reason, CIL, or BCCL, had been sold a system which was to a degree inappropriate for Indian geological conditions: namely the hardness of the coal, and the nature of the rock strata above the coal seams — sandstone, which tended to exert particular pressures on the roof supports. For example, the expert group convened to analyse the reasons for the poor results from mechanized faces commented:

Our operators have come across serious problems in operating and maintaining the equipment and almost invariably they tried to put the blame on the equipment. The Group confirms that a large number of equipment were not satisfactory. However the Group cannot but remark that inexperienced workmen are tempted to find fault with the tools. It must, however, be admitted that our operators faced unnecessary and avoidable constraints due to poor performance of the equipment. In fact, they had to devote more time and energy in keeping the equipment in running order rather than concentrate on working the faces as they otherwise could have done.

The Group is of the opinion that selection of the equipment is not satisfactory in a number of cases. (Expert group, 1984, p. 34).

DIVISION AND SOLIDARITY: UNDERSTANDING THE PERFORMANCE OF THE POWERED-SUPPORT FACES

We have seen that a real, practical, political and technical problem exists at Moonidih. A crucial modernization programme which spearheads the general modernization of the coal sector, on which the capacity of the coal industry to meet ever-incresing demand for coal from consumers and industry depends, is apparently faltering. On that there is agreement. But the explanations of this problem differ drastically. What then can the general approach on offer in this volume contribute to an understanding of the situation? How far and in what ways is the poor performance of the powered-support faces explicable in terms of the patterning of social relationships within Bharat Coking Coal Ltd, or Coal India Ltd, and the other associated organizations involved in the modernization? Is it possible to shed light on the problem through a consideration of structures of trust, distrust, solidarity and estrangement, perceived similarity, or apparent differences? We maintain that it is possible, to a degree. But first a few words of caution.

Precisely because of its practical significance the problem at Moonidih has been thoroughly researched by highly experienced and professional experts — BMC consultants, and the Government of India Expert Group. These experts have enormously more technical knowledge of mining and mine planning and technology than the author. The contribution of this analysis, if it has one, is not to question, or even add to, these expert analyses, but to place them in a perspective which their very professionalism and familiarity may obscure. Nevertheless the following analysis depends crucially on the work and involvement of these various expert groups, and is not intended to replace their findings, but, as in a kaleidoscope, to re-arrange these basic ingredients in a new shape. The focus of this analysis is not the origins of the performance problems, but the reasons for their persistence in the face of so much expert analysis.

The analysis recommended in this volume consists of a consideration of a number of work structures:

(1) How are social relationships within the work organization structured so as to form patterns of solidarity, exclusion: insiders and outsiders?
(2) What consequences do these structures of social relationships within

the work organization have for processes within and across these structures? In particular what consequences do they have for levels of trust, and for the smooth and reasonably accurate transmission of communications?

(3) What consequence do they have for the development of perceived structures of similar and opposed interests?

It will be recalled that in the previous case study of the LFB it was argued that there were real consequences for trust, perceived interests and communication stemming from the inadvertent structuring of the watch with the station officer as an isolated work and management unit. We shall now consider whether anything remotely similar is going on at Moonidih. We shall organize the analysis in two parts.

THE PROBLEM IS THE EXPLANATION

If we consider the explanations on offer from the various experts not as they are presented in their own terms, as right or wrong, but as phenomena in their own right, if, as it were, we refrain from being drawn into the constant argument about which side is correct, and which misguided, then some obvious patternings of the sort we are concerned with, emerge.

The explanations themselves are highly structured, in terms of their ownership. That is why it is possible to speak of 'sides'. The explanations reflect, and are clearly seen by their advocates and protagonists to reflect, different groups, different interests. The explanations reflect and articulate, structured differences. Even if one didn't know which people held which view of the causes of the poor levels of performance, it would still be obvious, from the reports themselves, that there were two different, opposed and competing explanations. These are not just different but complementary: they actually attack each other's base assumptions. One argues the technology is inappropriate; the other asserts that it is being misused, or even abused, or wrongly used and maintained.

Behind the differences, however, there are similarities in the two forms of explanation. The similarity is one of mistrust — mistrust of people as members of categories or sides. This is emphatically not to suggest that individuals involved mistrusted each other. The reverse is in fact true: the working relationships between and among the BMC consultants and Moonidih management are good; there is obvious respect between individual CIL officers and ODA officers; genuine and obvious honesty between Department of Coal officials and British manufacturers or BMC consultants.

But what is being suggested here is that at the level of explanation, both theories of both 'sides' carried assumptions about the nature of the people

oppositional rhetoric of distrust that is evident,
l, secondly, for actual working efficiency. The
n the working system — which may well be so
se of the expression 'overall working system'
reduces working efficiency. These 'breaks' occur
usterings, and within them. Both are counterpro-
hese two consequences are related in that the
is demonstrated in each group's explanation of the
What separates the explanations is not necessarily
out the interpretation, which is couched in terms of
clusterings generate. So the explanations of the
s products of the problem, and serve to perpetuate
working system fractured? Firstly it is obvious that
discrete organizations involved in the projects, with
s and objectives. In India there are: the Department
Ministry of Energy, in Delhi; Coal India Ltd, Calcutta,
Ltd, Dhanbad, and Moonidih management itself. In
as Development Administration, The Department of
manufacturers, British Mining Consultants, The British
thora of interested parties would be hard to organize
ational system. Yet such an achievement is essential to
vement of the project's goals. In fact, however, these
rganizations with their differing goals, do tend to cluster
i-modal, national foci.

rganizations are differentiated in terms of the nature of
d their responsibility for, the project, from their UK
d this coalescence of organizations is extremely important
's conception of itself, and of the other. The apparent
ternally ('us') breeds confidence within, and a shared view
and its problems, and is contrasted with a heterogeneity
') which encourages distrust.

organizations are essentially concerned with supply aid,
technology, with supplying consultancy. They are experts
he Indian organizations are concerned with receiving aid,
nology, and with using it. They are receivers, users and
though there is no doubt at all that all parties want the
n programme to succeed, and no suggestion here of the nature
s' commitment or motivation; structurally there is a difference
dian/receiver/user organizations, on the one hand, and UK/
lier/expert organizations on the other. Without knowing any
ould be possible to predict that with this imbalance between the
clusterings, their very unbalanced dependency would generate

involved on the other side. It might usefully be described as an institutionalized suspicion. On the Indian side the suspicion concerned the motives of
British manufacturers and experts (very clearly stated in the expert report),
and their understandable concern to sell their technology. Just how neutral
were they? Had they allowed their interest in selling to overcome their
more neutral, balanced role as advisers? Were the current explanations of
the problem in terms of poor maintenance, or management attitude,
actually attempts to shift responsibility away from where it properly lay? It
would be no exaggeration to say that this view was held, and held strongly,
at every level of CIL and the Department of Coal. In answer to the
question: 'How do you explain the poor output figures?', the answer was
always: the shearers were underpowered, the supports not able to cope
with the particular, diagonal pressures caused by the sandstone roof.

The other explanation also carried suspicion — about the competence
and motivation of the users of the technology, or more broadly, of the
organizational system within which the technology was deployed. Again
this view was extremely pervasive and widespread. It did not mean attacks
on actual individuals, any more than the alternative theory described
above. It was institutional in origin and institutional in target. Essentially
each view was suspicious of the 'other' as a concept, while endlessly able to
make exceptions for the individuals actually involved in both sides. But
these exceptions, however numerous and however readily acknowledged,
did not constitute a substantial alternation of the base, institutionalized,
suspicion.

The explanations themselves then, regardless of their relationship to
'the truth', demonstrated some of the key qualities this analysis identifies as
critical: they are, on the one hand, internally solidaristic and uniform, but,
on the other hand, externally highly differentiated. Their very internal
cohesion and popularity contrasts vividly with their external competitiveness. While the vast majority, if not all, Indian commentators see things
one way, the vast mass of UK consultants see the same things very
differently. And these differences are structurally opposed: they provide a
critique of each other's basic assumptions by questioning the motivation
and/or competence of the people concerned — not as individuals, but as
representatives of opposed systems. Furthermore these explanations
involve a key feature: the definition of certain groups — and their
representatives — as untrustworthy, as so contaminated by their membership of a defined category and the interests this must carry, as to be
rendered structurally suspect. However close the relationship, however
intimate and straightforward personal relationships, the structural, institutionalized distrust continues to dominate definitions of events and definitions of problems.

Currently available explanations of the poor performance of the powered-support faces demonstrate an obvious, striking and significant opposition and partiality. The important feature of these explanations is that in themselves they articulate suspicion and distrust. In view of this, the arguments of each side are likely to be seen not in terms of their merits, but as positions in a bargaining encounter — not as contributions to a rational dialogue, but as contributions to a negotiation, as positions, strategies, moves in a game.

This has very important consequences. The most significant is that the capacity of all the parties, acting together, to achieve a satisfactory solution to the agreed problem is greatly reduced when discussed of suggestions is blocked by division and mistrust. In short, the available explanations block the possibility of a mutual, general and acceptable explanation.

All this is regardless of truth. We have deliberately refrained from assessing the relative merits of the various explanations because the important point is not their truth, but their opposition, and, consequently, their significance for representing and articulating, opposition of interests, and therefore, for blocking mutual resolution. In short, the opposition of explanations, blocks the possibility of an explanation which could allow both parties to agree and act together. It is almost as if what was important here was not what each group said (for one or other may well have identified the problem) but the ability of both groups to speak together. What is important is not the problem itself, but the inability of both parties to share a conception of the problem, and an approach to, its resolution — to move from negotiation and bargaining (the perceived opposition of interests) to mutual problem solving. Why is it then that the two 'sides' have such difficulty in working together to define and resolve problems?

At a very early stage of the research a thoughtful and experienced manager from one of the UK suppliers remarked that what was unusual and perplexing about the Moonidih project, and its poor performance, was not that things went wrong, for they always went wrong, somehow, but what happened when things went wrong. Somehow, problems, errors, difficulties, were not well corrected. Indeed they may even be compounded. The system did not seem to be easily able to learn.

The system was very poor at self-correction. This is a critical, and highly perceptive point, for it identified an element which is notably lacking in the project, but which the opposed rhetoric described above overlooked: the critical feature of the project is the way in which — for one reason or another — the various parties to the project interrelate so as to achieve the objectives of the project. As the analysis of explanations for failure discussed above suggest, despite the fact that the various parties are working together on the project, in important ways they are not working

together. ...
ment on an ...
intense indi...
particularly ...
possibility of ...
vity which co...
'system' so as ...
sitions, of intere...

In Chapter 1 ...
principle of the o...
an organization in...
and pursue a variet...
consider the bounda...
tion finishes and an...
structured difference...
consider the Moonidih...
self-correct, and the fa...
mutually opposed theor...
and competence of 'ideal-...
to ask: how far, if at all, is...
work organization? The an...
involved here, but many, a...
overall collection of parties...
that is responsible for the de...
above.

The organization of the M...
ways. There are two importan...
project system is 'fractured', an...
system is on the one hand differe...
are defined as different objectives...
in, and authority for, the success o...
tiated groups coalesce and cluster in...
process of overlapping occurs wher...
located within one country are defi...
those that cluster in the other. So it i...
important, but the similarities which t...
structurally different, possibly even oppo...
process of perceived internal homogeneit...
neity in the case of the LFB. And we hav...
between groups.

The consequences of this fracturing of...
for the development of group perceptio...

development of the sort of ...
as described above — an...
existence of 'breaks' with...
severe as to make the ...
inapplicable — certainly ...
between the two major c...
ductive to efficiency. ...
distrust that is generated ...
identified inefficiencies ...
the object of analysis, ...
the very attitudes the ...
problem are themselve...
it. How is the overall ...
there are a great man...
different philosophie...
of Coal, part of the N...
Bharat Coking Coal ...
the UK, The Overs...
Trade, the various ...
Council. Such a pl...
into a single, oper...
the efficient achie...
various different ...
but around two, ...
The Indian o...
their role in, a...
counterparts. A...
for each cluste...
homogeneity in...
of the project ...
without ('them...
So, the U...
with supplyin...
and givers. ...
receiving te...
learners. A...
modernizati...
of individua...
between In...
donor/supp...
details, it ...
two sets o...

attitudes of scepticism whereby users would doubt the objectivity and quality of the giver's advice, or the technology supplied; and the givers would doubt the manner in which the products/advice were used. And this is exactly what we find.

The structural imbalance comes about because each national group needs the other — to give to, or to receive from — but yet this relationship itself is not equal. It may be as worthy to give as to receive but it surely is not the same, what ever the product being exchanged may be. Secondly, the different sorts of contribution to the overall programme involve unequal degrees of experienced responsibility for the success of the programme. Their 'ownership' of, or relationship to, the problem and the project is very different, yet interconnected. But the differences, allied to the fact that they mutually interact, may create systematic problems of mutual attitude. For Moonidih management, output levels are a major, national issue, a subject of newspaper editorials, of the Chairman of CIL's personal interest, and a major issue in their career development. For UK suppliers and consultants the success of the project certainly matters, but in a different sort of way. However committed they may be individually, they don't have to live with it; their careers aren't dependent on it; they aren't responsible for it. Their responsibility is to supply good advice, machinery, training; the Moonidih managers on the other hand are responsible for making all these resources work — and their careers may depend on it.

But what is at issue here is not individual motivation or commitment, but the fact that the various organizations involved in the project are (a) discrete and heterogenous and also (b) nationally homogeneous in the nature of their involvement and their responsibility for project performance; for this gives rise to what members of each group define as a structured difference of interest in the project. This is not to say that each group regards the other as uninterested in the project success. This is not the case. But they see the others as having a different *sort* of interest in the programme. And so interests and motives are systematically constructed.

This differentiation and re-integration of the contributing groups to the project has two consequences as noted earlier. It encourages the development of an oppositional rhetoric which articulates these differences — gives them voice — by saying, for the receivers, 'we are not confident in the impartiality of your advice, we fear your role as manufacturers may have contaminated your judgement', and by saying for the givers, 'we doubt how well you are using and applying our advice and our technology'. If things don't work out, it follows that this is because of the nature of the advice/technology, or because of the way in which it is applied (maintained). Such theories explain the disappointment in terms of available, 'common-sense' definitions and knowledge. As they explain, they legitimate, by transferring blame. They thus articulate the fracturing of the system, while exacerbating it. But there is another consequence, of equal importance: the nature of the system actually influences its effectiveness. The differentiation of the total project system causes real problems of communication and hence of efficiency; and the nature of working relationships within parts of the system also strongly influences the outcome of the project.

The two opposed explanations differ in content, as we have seen but share a basic form: the distrust of the other's performance of their essential (giver/receiver) role. Ironically, although in a sense part of the problem, these theories also accurately describe the problem if one puts them together and moves beyond the surface considerations — maintenance, training, geology — and asks: Why did these things go wrong? Frequently this question must be answered in terms of the inability of all the elements of the total system to work together: to ask for information, to supply information, to transmit information, or to receive and process it thoroughly. Thus to describe the poor output from the mechanized faces in terms of geology is not to go far enough, for this offers a technological or geological gloss on what is, essentially, an organizational problem: why were the geological specifications not accurate enough, or not acted on? These are system, or human issues, not geological ones. But these practical, efficiency consequences of the lack of system integration are themselves defined in turn in terms of the oppositional rhetoric described above. Thus reality and appearance mutually fuel each other. The authors of the Expert Group Report appreciated this clearly enough. They wrote:

> There appears to be a continuous difference of opinion between the users and the equipment suppliers with respect to merits of the equipment. There was hardly any positive approach. Such attempt to transfer blame on each other is not conducive to evolve a tolerable policy of after-sales service, speedy procurement of spares and their indigenous manufacture. Somewhere and somehow there has got to be an understanding of each other's problems which was badly wanting. (Expert Group, 1984, p. 39)

All the major reasons advanced by UK and Indian commentators: appropriateness of technology, geology, maintenance, spares, management, can be seen as symptoms of the less-than-satisfactory operation of the system overall, of one section not working smoothly with another. It suggests that a satisfactory, aided programme of modernization presents major and serious difficulties at the organizational level, as well as at many other levels. Members of both 'sides' identified difficulties within the Indian management of the programme. The UK commentators tend to focus, sensibly, on the importance of appropriate management structures to support the longwall project. BMC authors wrote, in a major assessment of progress:

> Of equal importance is the ability of line management to organise, supervise and direct all operations, with the attention to detail demanded by highly mechanised longwall mining. BMC is of the opinion that the management structure and the management approach at Moonidih must be reviewed in the light of the specific needs of mechanised longwall mining. There is a significant difference between the management of low output, low technology mines and high technology mechanised mines. (BMC, 1984, p. 12).

A not dissimilar point is made by the authors of the expert group report when they comment adversely on the long delays between selection of equipment and the actual start-up of a face which results in equipment being installed which is already out-of-date. It is reported that there has been as long as 5 or 6 years delay between concept of a project and final installation. The expert group wonder if the many stages betwen plan and execution are necessary, if anything could be done to short-circuit the process, and if it is sensible for a new appointee somewhere senior in the planning hierarchy to be able to overturn the lengthy deliberations of a planning team. In essence, these authors are making the same point as the BMC authors: that the overall system needs to be adapted to cope with the new requirements. It is not a question of individual's competence, but of the way in which decisions are made, the ways in which change is instigated, the distribution of responsibilities and authorities. For example, is it practically sensible for planning to remain a centralized function within the Indian coal sector? Elsewhere, for example within the UK, projects are prepared by the operating area in which the project will take place. Responsibility for planning the project is thus devolved to the end-user. Practical difficulties with the project are thus identified early. There is no separation of planning and execution, as seems to occur in the case of Moonidih. The crucial issue of ownership of the problem and the solution — i.e. the project overall and the installation of the new technology — is clearly located with those with responsibility for making the project work, who are also the project designers. In the Indian case, these functions are crucially separated, thus potentially introducing at the same time, the possibility of inappropriate technical solutions, in situations where users may not be disposed to regard these technical solutions, however good they may be, as their own.

But if the nature and functioning of the complete modernization system — including its UK elements — is an essential factor in the capacity of the system to identify and resolve problems, then it becomes critical that this question of overall system efficiency receives analysis and attention. Is this in fact the focus of current efforts to resolve the much-publicized problems of the programme? Not surprisingly, it is not.

THE SOLUTION AS PART OF THE PROBLEM

Efforts to resolve the problems identified as contributing to the overall poor output figures, while entirely sensible within their own terms of reference, tend to be excessively technical, and insufficiently system-oriented. They are, as it were, firefighting measures, rather than fire-prevention.

We have argued here that the problem at Moonidih will not be resolved until the way in which problems and solutions are identified, defined and faced alters. Essentially, the critical change will involve the development of a total, integrated system, including the external suppliers, consultants and trainers, and, most importantly, the development of a more effective Indian system, incorporating all interested parties, in a manner which is able to respond appropriately and at the appropriate level, to the project and its problems. In brief, the issue here is not a question of identification of the problem, but of ownership of it. As things stand, those who experience, those who resolve, and those who identify the problems at Moonidih have very different degrees and forms of responsiblity for, and authority over and ownership of, the problems. This has been noted before, by the ex chairman-cum-managing Director of CMPDI, who wrote of the emergence of large, modernized mines, 'there will be a need to ensure management development in synchronism. Starting from the organization structure, wage systems, multi-disciplinary operation and supervisory skills to ware-housing, maintenance management information systems, construction and cost monitoring — a radically different system has to be developed'. But such structural initiatives are not in fact the response to problems. Instead what happens is understandably, piecemeal correction.

The major solution involves the consultancy activities, at Moonidih, of BMC consultants, often managers and planners seconded from the NCB. These peoples' commitment and professionalism and involvement are enormous, working long hours with tremendous enthusiasm — and with great success. Their activities are unquestionably highly effective. For example one report shows that prior to the arrival of a BMC trouble-shooting team of practical experts, average daily output for the two preceding months were 415 tonnes per day and 582 tonnes per day. But during the last eight days of the team's visit, average daily production was 747 tonnes.

A similar pattern was apparent on other occasions, when the presence and activity and enthusiasm of BMC consultants contributed greatly to the overcoming of difficulties and to increased output. For example, during the author's recent visit to Moonidih, three BMC consultants were seconded to Moonidih working on the installation of a new powered-support face. During their visit a transformer went off, thus losing power to the new face. With nothing to do, the consultants visited the other powered face, which at that time was temporarily out-of-action. Immediately the consultants went into action, sorted out the problems, shouted at a few lounging miners, motivated the supervisors, and by the time they left the face, the shearer was moving and a cut had been achieved. The consultants returned to the surface, went straight to the office of the general manager and informed him of the problems underground and arranged for the supply of much-delayed spares. They returned to the guest house, and a couple of hours later, the under-managers from the face arrived to report that they had achieved, remarkably, a second cut. The significance of this is that the managers reported to the consultants; the consultants intervened with the general manager; and it was the consultants who effectively took over the management of the powered face and the shift. The results were highly impressive. Of particular interest was the close relationship between consultants and shift managers. But, ironically,.however, necessary such remedial activity in the short term (and however understandable on the human level) on the system level this sort of solution exacerbates the problem, rather than resolves it. It exemplifies and reinforces the division noted earlier: giver/expert versus receiver learner. It exacerbates the tendency for users to see suppliers/consultants as responsible for solutions, it exacerbates the tendency for the system to persist uninterrogated, and to be salvaged by piecemeal adjustments. It leaves unanalysed the causes of the problems. Why were miners lounging about before the consultants arrived? Why were the shift managers apparently unable on their own to exercise authority? Why had senior management not yet ensured that the necessary spares were available? These and many other questions are raised by this incident. But none of them will be identified or addressed as a result of it. Despite the heroic work of the consultants on this and many other occasions, which will no doubt result in the sort of increased output figures mentioned earlier, these outcomes will be temporary and will do nothing to make the need for more visits in the future unnecessary. Systems and base assumptions, operationalized in such patterns of problem identification and expert resolution, will persist uninterrogated. Dependence of user on giver is, if anything increased. Both sides are locked into a pattern of unreciprocal dependence, associated with the structuring of differential involvement in the project, and with bodies of legitimating theory and knowledge, which ensure the continuation of the very problems both sides wish to eliminate, but which persist because of the very way they are defined — in terms of the assumptions inherent in oppositional rhetorics, which themselves encapsulate the very realtionships of dependence (giver/receiver).

4

Work — community, politics and informal organization

So far in this book we have argued that a sociological interest in work of the widest sort, which is not restricted to current problematics (the origins of the design of work within capitalism) but addresses a wider range of work issues — for example of the sort described in the two previous chapters, neither of which are amenable to the analytic framework established by Bravermania — such as a concern to understand work processes and outcomes in general, is greatly assisted by a study of the manner in which work organizations are 'fractured' by patterns of social relationships. The two proceding chapters have shown how work organizations are patterned by distinctive and inadvertent structures of social relationships which play an important part in organizational dynamics and efficiency. These patterns consist of social groupings of inclusion and exclusion, within which members establish at least an element of their total identities, share a work-based morality (what things are and should be like, who is a hero, who a villain; which contains shared myths and knowledge) and interrelate more intensely and meaningfully than they do with outsiders. These groupings consist essentially of boundaries: within these boundaries — social, moral, cultural — members experience a marked differentiation from, even opposition to, specified outsiders. Understanding these patternings, their significance for those within and those without, and their implications for trust, confidence, the perception of shared interests, is important to any understanding of patterns of overall, organizational solidarity or differentiation and the behaviours that follow from these.

These outcomes can, as we have seen, be of various sorts. We considered two: resistance to senior managers' policies, even to the law; and organizational inability to respond effectively to public and conspicuous problems.

Work organizations work through working together. The formal differentiation of the organization's structures is, in theory, designed effectively to achieve the organization's goals. Clearly therefore, the actual differentiation or fracturing of the organization's structures is likely to contribute to all activities within, and all outcomes of, the organization. It is likely therefore to be of the greatest significance to the sociology of work. And this is what we find.

Our analysis of work structures has so far been concerned with two case studies. These illustrate the essential importance of the approach. But they leave a number of more general questions concerned with the general aspects of the analysis, largely unexplored: *why* and *how* are work relationships structured? In what sorts of case are these structures causally significant? In what ways may work relationships be structured? In short, we need a consideration of causes, forms, and consequences of the patterning of work relationships.

Luckily, if predicatably, we find that in fact much of the sociology of work has been concerned, in one way or another, with our object of analysis. Indeed it can be said that it represents the major object of interest of the sociology of work, although often approached in such a variety of ways as to mask the fact that a single issue is being discussed. If, however, we define our object of analysis as widely as possible to include, for example, the question of class structures and class consciousness at work (for what is class if not the most significant form of group structuring, and what is class consciousness but the extreme exemplification of internal group solidarity and external estrangement and distrust?) then there can be no doubt that class structuration and the emergence of class consciousness represent important examples of the processes under review here.

The sociology of work offers many insights on these issues as we shall see, although not necessarily in a coherent fashion. We shall add the coherence.

However, by talking of the sociology of work we are avoiding an issue: there is no sociology of work. There is sociology, and there is work but the former is not homogeneous in its treatment of the latter, and sociologically, the latter is not homogeneous either. Sociologically, there are a number of discrete but overlapping sub-disciplines which define their subject-matter in terms of work activities and institutions, e.g. the sociology of organization, of occupations, of professions, of industry, of industrial relations. All this need not matter but simply be another indication of the strange, arcane, hopelessly 'academic' nature of the discipline. But for our purposes there is an implication: the different sub-disciplines treat the object of our analysis in significantly different ways, thus producing the diversity mentioned above.

It is possible to distinguish three distinct forms of approach to the sociological analysis of work structuring. Each of these constitutes the major focus of one characteristic sub-discipline: work and community studies; occupational studies; and organizational studies which include theories of the class implications of the differentiation of organization work forces. Each will be considered in turn. Each approach offers a distinctive and characteristic conceptualization of how work relationships are structured, and their consequences.

WORK AND COMMUNITY

During the 1950s and early 1960s British industrial sociologists researched community at work. This is no longer an item on the research agenda; indeed probably most students of the sociology of work in the mid 1980s will never even consider the issue. The reasons for this are interesting in themselves, for we tend to research what we regard as surprising — suprisingly present or surprisingly absent. The recent but late enthusiasm for community studies reflected sociologists' surprise at, and concern for, a vanishing form of work/community connection. In the 1980s we no longer regard the absence of such a phenomena as requiring explanation. This tells us something about us, and a lot about the times we live in.

Studies of work and community were concerned with two overlapping phenomena; communities at work, and work within communities. The first occurs when people who work together choose to establish a form of relationship among themselves which can sensibly be described as an occupational community. They may or may not live together. If they do it is because they choose to, as a result of their work-based closeness. Usually, however, they do not live together.

But whether they live together or not spatially, they live together socially and culturally. they inhabit the same world of meaning and identity; share a language, a vocabulary of symbols, knowledge of the work world, a world of taken-for-granted and shared references, mythic figures, incident, jokes — in short a culture. This theme is treated helpfully, and at much greater length, in a companion volume in the *Key Ideas* Series — Tony Cohen's *The Symbolic Construction of Community* (Ellis Horwood, Chichester, 1985). Joining such an occupational community involves not simply or primarily learning the formal procedures and skills, but becoming an insider to the highly restricted cultural code which is incomprehensible to the outsider, and which is not open to entry until the newcomer has demonstrated his/her willingness to accept the authority of the community, has demonstrated his/her appreciation that entry is dependent on the approval of insiders, and has been systematically humiliated by his/her ignorance and outsider status. Many occupational communities involve institutionalized initiation ceremonies which exemplify the transition from stranger/outsider to accepted member of the community. As well as demonstrating to the sociologist the strength of the work-based cultures, these initiations demonstrate to the recruit that s/he has achieved entry, and by virtue of the pain involved in gaining entry, they make membership itself that much more significant and valued. Examples of such occupational communities include: the police, musicians, printers, carnival workers, firefighters, and many others. (See, for example, Perkins (1984) for a thorough catalogue of studies of such communities).

The second form of the phenomenon — work within communities — is probably the more familiar version. This is the often idealized object of sociological and more general nostalgia — the pit village, the fishing village, the railway town, the steel community. The forms vary but the essence remains: a community that lived together in geographical or social isolation also worked together. Industrial sociology contains some classic studies of this classic phenomenon. Their very titles display their subject matter: *Coal is Our Life* (Dennis *et al.*, 1956), *The Fishermen* (Tunstall, 1969), *The Railroader* (Cottrell, 1940). In its pure form this type of occupational community involves working-class occupations of a particular traditional, manual, sort.

When researchers refer to occupational communities they usually define them in terms of three interrelated ingredients which occur regardless of whether the community is geographical or not: relationships, identity and values. 'Members of occupational communities do not attempt to separate their work and non-work lives: . . . the most important feature of this is that they prefer to be friends with people who do the same work . . . A colleague is someone who inhabits the same normative and associational world' (Salaman, 1974, pp. 25–26).

Secondly, 'members of occupational communities see themselves in terms of their occupational role: their self-image is centred on their occupational role in such a way that they see themselves as printers, policemen, army officers . . . as people with specific qualities, interests and abilities' (Salaman, 1974). These work-based self-images will be a source of personal pride, and the qualities associated with them will be seen as personally achieved. the identity is earned, sometimes uncomfortably, often with difficulty, always at a cost. It is worth something.

Finally, members of such communities share a world of values, largely work-based and work-relevant, but not entirely. This *describes* the work world and the nature of the people who inhabit it (this process excludes most sorts of people, but defines key ones) and *prescribes* necessary and desirable behaviour. It is both a science and a morality.

Various factors have been adduced to explain the development and persistence of these phenomena (see Salaman, 1974; Perkins, 1984). Essentially, three factors have been identified: involvement in work tasks (for various reasons, often concerned with skill, danger or excitement); some degree of marginality, which makes relationships with outsiders undesirable or difficult: and the 'inclusiveness' of the work or organizatioal setting — i.e. anything which tends to create boundaries around those who work together, thus encouraging the development of relationships within while making relationships outside difficult (Salaman, 1974).

Clearly then an occupational community represents an extremely powerful version of the phenomenon we are discussing in this volume. When an occupational community occurs, it requires that people who work together live together, socially and culturally, and share a work-based identity. Studies of occupational communities are much more interested in describing what such communities are like (in terms of the three element listed above) than they are interested in explaining them, or in analysing their consequences. And they tend to explain occupational communities in terms of fortuitous combinations of determinants rather than to see such structures as to any degree responses to external factors. These analyses are somewhat passive, reflecting a form of sociological analysis which interpreted class analysis in terms of discovering and celebrating class life-styles (which were seen as the seed-beds for class attitudes) rather than seeking examples and origins of actions which could be regarded as cases of class action. Members are not seen as *constructing* social boundaries, but simply as enjoying them. Nevertheless such studies contribute to our analysis rich and thorough case studies of a particular convergence of work and non-work. These studies demonstrate the enormous potential of such a convergence; but in themselves they rarely analyse the implications of this potential for the work organization. In terms of our interests of this chapter in *why* work relations are fractured, *how* they are fractured and *what* consequences follow this fracturing, then community studies offer material for the second of these interests — *how* work relations are fractured, but relatively little on the first and third interests. Later we shall see that other approaches tend similarly to contribute to one of our interests but not to all of them.

However, the earlier work by this author mentioned above (Salaman, 1974) does attempt a classification of some of the factors responsible for the development of occupational communities, and we shall consider whether these three factors require modification in the light of contributions to our analysis from other areas of the sociology of work. However, some writers within this tradition have considered the implications of the phenomena (other than for the members). two consequences have been identified — one implicit, one explicit. The implicit consequence is a logical outcome of the existence of an occupational community: work matters far more than when an occupational community does not exist. If an occupational community means that people who work together — or who do the same work — share some of life together, then any threat to that work, or to the skills which it is seen by its practitioners to require, or to elements of the identity which is built upon practising these skills, or doing that job, will be experienced as critical. It follows that if such a threat is experienced as mattering, then all other things being equal, it will be resisted. Or, if not, it will require a proportionally greater degree of persuasion or pressure to persuade or force incumbents of the occupation to accept change. Already it is to be hoped that the alert reader will be able to make connections with the analysis of the London firefighters discussed earlier. For they display the three key elements of the occupational community and their response to the EO programme is all the stronger for its significance, as the firemen see it, for their work-based self-images as manly men whose work both demands and reflects their manlines, and for their pride in having achieved careers within the Brigade in the face of intense competition from their peers.

In short, the existence of an occupational community means that changes at work matter greatly to members of the community (who have personally identified with their work) *and* that members are more likely to resist such changes. It *may* also mean that they are more *able* to resist change. But this is a separate factor, and one to which we shall return. Certainly, however, the existence of an occupational community implicitly means that people involved will be more concerned, more identified with their work and therefore more concerned about any changes in their work. Clearly then this is potentially important in the development of work resistance and struggle. So far, however, our analysis has stopped short of suggesting that occupational communities are necessarily self-conscious interest groups. They can be; but they are not always. They are, however, a good base for such groups.

The second implication of occupational communities — or some sorts of occupational communities — has been suggested by Lockwood who, arguing that people tend to visualize the class divisions of their society in terms of vantage points of their particular locations and experience, seeks to classify, in somewhat idealized form, the various social milieux responsible, in general terms, for distinctive social imagery. To this end he classifies what he calls the 'traditional' worker, usually associated as he notes, with industries such as mining, docking, shipbuilding. Of such workers he writes that they:

> usually have a high degree of job involvement and strong attachments to primary work groups that possess a considerable autonomy from the technical and supervisory constraints. Pride in doing 'men's work' and a strong sense of shared occupational experience make for feelings of fraternity and comradeship which are expressed through a distinctive occupational culture . . . Shaped by occupational solidarities and communal sociability the proletarian social consciousness is centred on an awareness of 'us' in contradistinction to 'them' who are not part of 'us'. 'Them' are bosses, managers, white collar workers and, ultimately, the public authorities of the larger society. (Lockwood, 1975, p. 198)

This is an important new stage in the argument. In fact there are really two stages.

First, Lockwood argues that the very solidarity and sense of personal identification — the 'them' and 'us' already identified in the two case studies in the previous chapter — constitutes a significant basis for conflict because of the way it divides and integrates the social world. As he and others have noted, if one sees society, or the world, divided into two camps then relationships between these two camps are more likely to be defined in terms of opposition than if we see society divided into a number of different camps. Simply by increasing the numbers of perceived groups, the possibilities of a variety of relationships and alliances is introduced; and the nature of relationships between a number of different groups is likely to reflect their very multiplicity. Two groups can stand starkly opposed in terms of their mutual opposition; but many groups can differ more gradually, by degree of their differences.

Secondly, Lockwood argues that this polarization of the social world is important for its significance for class images. Members of traditional proletarian occupations, with their associated occupational communities are, as a consequence, likely to see society as divided into opposed classes. For Lockwood and later sociologists this is the important point: the significance of occupational communities as exemplars of the fracturing of work relationships lies in their impact on class attitudes. But this is wrong. It is true that these communities *can* be associated with traditional 'them' and 'us' notions of class, and even on occasion with related displays of class action. But this by no means exhausts their significance for conflict and opposition, as the two examples discussed earlier illustrate. Both cases involve opposition to programmes of planned change by collections of employees who see themselves as sharing — to varying degrees — interests and membership. Both cases involve the creation, or prior existence, of boundaries and demarcations which are certainly relevant to the development of a level of resistance, but which are in neither case class boundaries. In fact the strength of feeling of members of occupational communities, and their conviction that the social world is divided into categories of 'us' and 'them' represents a potential for opposition and resistance of numerous and various sorts on many dimensions. These may take class forms, they may not. There is no *a priori* reason for their necessarily doing so. They are just as likely to take forms which cross-cut class, which, far from expressing class interests, undermine or deny them.

OCCUPATIONAL STUDIES

Within the sociological analysis of occupations there is a tradition of analysis which speaks directly to our concerns in this chapter. This tradition involves the analysis of occupations or professions in terms of efforts by members to advance or defend their interests. Such an approach — occupations regarded as interest groups and analysed in terms of their 'political' behaviour — represents a significant development of our analysis of the causes, nature and consequences of the fracturing of work relationships. It is a development which is clearly relevant to our two case studies. For though neither of them are occupations, both involve a degree of 'political' action in that both involve levels of opposition to programmes of change. Up to now we have paid relatively little attention to the *consequences* of such structuring. Members of occupational communities, who were shown to represent a somewhat extreme example of the phenomenon under consideration here were seen to develop distinctive work-based identities, share a work-based culture and associate with each other. They were shown to inhabit a particular and demarcated work-based social and cultural space, clearly set apart from the outside and outsiders. But members of such communities were seen somewhat *passively*, as recipients, participants, members — not as actively doing anything as a result of their membership, except enjoying it, and living within its assumptions. However, towards the end of the previous section our analysis began, through a consideration of Lockwood's work to move towards the possibility that such patterns of work relations could constitute a powerful basis for joint action. 'The degree to which a group has developed a strong occupational consciousness is the degree to which it is capable of increasing its political power and material rewards . . . The division of labour between groups that stand in a hierarchical relationship to each other is always a source of interest-based occupational conflict' (Krause, 1971, pp. 85–86). This passage identifies the main elements of the approach: occupations inhabit different structural positions on which the perception of differentiated interests can be developed. Members of occupations develop occupational consciousness and ideologies which represent them, and which describe their shared conception of interests and what needs to be done to achieve them.

In fact there are difficulties with this approach, as will be discussed below. Essentially these difficulties revolve around two issues: the conditions under which people who do the same work not only define themselves as sharing a common predicament, develop a shared culture and work-based identities (as discussed in the Chapters 2 and 3) but also organize and mobilize to try to achieve these interests. In short, under what conditions does the fracturing of work relationships and the development of notions of 'them' and 'us' lead to a shared 'consciousness' — with its implication of perceived interest to be pursued actively? Secondly, when people at work do develop a consciousness of interests and a shared determination to achieve them, what factors influence their *capacity* to achieve them and what tactics are likely to be used successfully? We shall return to both these issues. In fact the tradition of analysis under consideration here — occupational studies — has more to say on the first than the second, which is more fruitfully treated within other traditions of analysis, discussed later in the chapter.

But although there are difficulties with the analysis of occupations as interest groups, this approach has also considerable heuristic ability. Certainly it is not able to explain *why* and *when* occupations, or other collections of workmates or colleagues, develop a consciousness of shared interests and a preparedness to act in pursuit of them. But it is very powerful in its capacity to illuminate what happens when they do. 'Occupations and professions have now been seen as self-interested, self-conscious sectors that use ideologies and power inherent in their role' (Krause, 1971, p. 102). This is particularly applicable to professions. For these occupations represent the prime example of occupations which have managed to achieve status and power and income through the deployment of a number of political strategies. Several dominant occupations (professions) have managed to attain positions of incredible power within Western societies. They have achieved this through a number of strategies — for example, the establishment and dissemination of an ideology which stresses the uniqueness of the professions, the unsuitability of conventional control systems, the inapplicability of normal customer/expert relations, the essential trustworthiness of professionals, etc., the achievement of internal professional control, licencing and colleague evaluation, the legalization of professional monopoly (McKinlay, 1973).

The sociological understanding of professions has gained enormously from the utilization of an approach which regards them as political phenomena, as interest groups. For now their very professional status itself is explained not in terms of instrinsic aspects of the work (for this is to confuse professional rhetoric with sociological analysis) but in terms of their success at insisting on the uniqueness of their work, while, 'there is no logical basis for distinguishing between so-called professions and other occupations'. (McKinlay, 1973, p. 65) In fact the claimed distinctiveness serves the interests of the professionals and is encouraged and sustained by their practices.

Such an analysis has the great merit of demystifying professions — or any other occupation — by insisting on moving beyond the claims and the rhetoric to analysing where such claims come from, whose interests they serve, what their consequences are.

We have seen, in Chapter 2 and 3, that the analyses there of the claims and convictions of the protagonists in the Moonidih modernization, and of the London Fire Brigade firemen and station officers, both rely on a determination to treat these statements not as reflections of reality, but as reflections of the situation and concerns of the parties involved. That *they* see them as truth, which they undoubtedly do, should be taken to indicate the close connection between rhetoric and experienced situation, not their essential truth. And it certainly should not require us, the sceptical sociologists, to accept them in the terms in which they are presented. In Chapter 2 it was also noted that statements by protagonists — for example the station officers — tended not simply and only to represent an interest position, but to assert the functional importance to the effective execution of their duties of the conditions they desired. Like members of professions, the station officers argued not in terms of personal preferences but in terms of what were claimed to be the requirements of efficiency which, they insisted, they were best placed, as practitioners, to recognize. 'When an occupation attempts to advance its interest in the society, it almost never admits that this is what is taking place. Instead, claims are made that greater power for the group is "in the public interest" . . . To define the public interest as the same as the interest of one's group is a privilege of power' (Krause, 1971, pp. 91, 98). It will be seen, then, how the approach under discussed in this section has contributed to the analyses presented in the previous chapters.

Secondly, such an approach contributes to an understanding of organizational process. The approach not only helps explain *how* occupations, or workmates achieve increased status and power; it also explains how the struggle *between* such groups can contribute to developments within organizations. There are many examples of this, all of which show how occupational groups seek to influence organizational decision-making to their advantage. At its most mundane, this commonplae phenomenon is evident when different departments within an organization struggle for scarce resources, or seek to avoid a proposed cut in budget or staff by insisting on the primacy of their particular contribution. More interestingly, a number of writers have seen the development of new work technologies, new work systems, new markets and new products as vehicles for occupational or work-group advancement who use the opportunity of such advances to advance their interests. For example, Armstrong has developed this line of argument with respect to scientific management itself. Developing the work of Layton, Armstrong argues that:

> scientific management, in its criticisms of traditional supervision and in its claim that the administration of labour should be monopolised by the 'planning department', was a product of the 'ideology of engineering'. This, in turn, was an expression of the resentment of the American mechanical engineers of the day, hitherto accustomed to the ownership or substantial control of small jobbing machine shops, at their subordination in growing bureaucratic organisations as industrial concentration proceeded. (Armstrong, 1984, p. 98)

Numerous studies within the tradition under discussion here support this basic point, that organizational structure and organizational process both constrain and are determined by the power relationships between occupational categories: 'how a specialist group defines its task, how it protects its identity by the development of a system of values and generally how it links itself with the activities of interdependent specialities' (Pettigrew, 1975, p. 260). This study by Pettigrew is an interesting example of many such studies, for two reasons. First, Pettigrew's analysis of intra-occupational power relations within the confines of a major organizational change (a decision to purchase and install new computers) is remarkably pertinent to our interest in the nature and functions of those ideologies which are generated by groups who inhabit the same demarcated organizational space, as illustrated in the previous chapters.

Secondly, he has useful things to say about the sorts of strategies developed and deployed by such groups. Pettigrew notes that when a new speciality or group — new 'outsiders', new 'them' — enter an organizational arena their claims for status, power and functions are likely to be regarded by established groups as expansionist and illegitimate. As he notes, a typical response from established groups is to accuse the new ones of incompetence and encroachment. This of course is exactly what we find in the two cases discussed in Chapters 2 and 3. Station officers insist on the incompetence of women, and of those who support the policy of recruiting women; each 'side' in the Moonidih modernization accuses the other in broadly similar terms. Pettigrew continues, and anticipates our case studies, to note that:

> The older group may also attempt to invoke a set of fictions about itself to protect the core of its expertise. These fictions or myths, supported by intra-group solidarity, can provide the established group with a comforting self-image to help meet and adapt to pressures for outside . . . As one group seeks power and the other survival, each will develop a set of stereotypes and misconceptions about the other. (Pettigrew, 1975, p. 260)

This should sound familiar. This study and others within this tradition (see, for example, Elliott, 1975) usefully describe the content and the function of the ideologies which are generated by those who share, and compete within, a demarcated work space.

These ideologies as noted earlier, describe and prescribe. They offer mythic pasts, and golden futures. They encourage those within as well as exhorting those outside. They articulate the very social demarcations which give them existence by defining the virtues of 'us' in contrast to the inadequacies of 'them'.

The point is not to define these ideologies as false or dishonest. Such judgements should not be within the preserve of the sociologist. The point is rather *not* to accept unquestioningly, the veracity of such statements, but to be indifferent to questions of truth, and focus instead on the relationship between convictions and interests: 'Professional ideologies result from the need to make sense of recurrent work problems and tasks within a particular organisation and career setting and of the need to present the work to others in the community, to compete for attention, control and resources' (Elliott, 1975, p. 275).

However, despite the advantages that may accrue from the approach considered in this section, two key questions, identified earlier, remain. These concern consciousness and capacity/strategy. The first shall be addressed here; the second will be considered in the next section.

In the quotation from Krause offered earlier, Krause asserts that a group's 'occupational consciousness' is closely related to its capacity to increase its political power and material rewards. This may be true; in fact for Krause it *must* be true, for occupational consciousness is defined by Krause in terms of a determination and capacity to act politically. But this is not in fact very helpful. For though we want to know how groups operate when they act politically (and this approach *is* helpful here, with its conceptualization of occupational ideology) it is also important to know the circumstances under which occupational or work consciousness develops, and the circumstances under which such consciousness of interests can be realized. We shall refer to these as the problms of consciousness and problems of capacity.

But clearly we cannot deal with these issues exhaustively. The problem of consciousness constitutes *the* major issue in Marxist-inspired sociology. Here we can just hope to make some general points which pertain to the development of consciousness of shared interests among those who work together.

(1) First we must define consciousness in this context. We can do this by borrowing from definitions of class consciousness. Giddens, for example, in his definition of class consciousness notes how it involves a conception of class identity and class differentiation. This is a basic but not a very high level of consciousness; a higher level involves a 'perception of class unity . . . linked to a recognition of opposition of interest' (Giddens, 1982, p. 163). The final level, which is hardly an element of occupational consciousness, except where this becomes class consciousness, involves the determination radically to reorganize power within society.

Gidden's classification covers the phenomenon we are dealing with. It will be noted that his basic stage of consciousness (when applied to work groups rather than to classes) describes exactly the 'them' and 'us' distinction so clearly charcteristic of both the case studies; and we have also seen that this differentiation is indeed, on occasion, and under particular circumstances, vested with notions of opposition and conflict. But, it is also very clear, and we shall return to this below, that although these two stages ('them' and 'us' and the conception of opposed or conflicting interests between the differentiated categories) is clearly characteristic of our case studies (and of other cases discussed within the approaches under consideration in this chapter), the relationship between this level of work-based consciousness of shared interests and action of a collective sort in pursuit of these interests, is uncertain and tenuous. It happens, but not often.

Part of the explanation of this is revealed when we consider what is meant by 'opposition of interests'. This can cover a number of different circumstances, from full-blooded and total opposition on all fronts, to a much more selective opposition on a limited and partial series of issues. For example, in the case of the modernization of Moonidih, opposition was highly partial: both parties recognized the reality of shared interests in the endeavour, but of different approaches to it. Similarly in the case of the station officers, although it was common to question the management philosophy and objectives of senior officers, it was extremely rare for any station officer to question their seniors' professional, firefighting competence. Opposition in both cases was limited to certain issues, but did not spread to others.

Similarly, just as the extent and nature of experienced opposition relates uncertainly to the experience of identity and differentiation, so the opposition and conflict of interests relates uncertainly to the extent and nature of actions in pursuit of these interests. The more partial and particular the extent and form of conflicts of interest, the more likely that actions in defence or pursuit of these interests will be partial, even contradictory. In both the case studies, the protagonists concerned were not involved in total, organized and generalized campaigns of opposition. On the contrary, their actions were on the whole cooperative; their resistance was limited to systematic muttering, gossip, rumour-mongering.

The extent and form of opposed interests, and the extent and form of actions expressing such conflicts, vary. They cannot simply be assumed. Too frequently studies of occupations of the sort considered in this section simply assume what should be the starting point of their analyses: the extent to which people who work together experience themselves as sharing interests, and the forms of action which followed from this.

(2) Secondly we must consider the sorts of factors which encourage consciousness of shared interests among those who share work identity, culture and relations which are experienced as opposed to the interests of others.

It is usual here to note those aspects of shared work experience which are likely to encourage consciousness of interests, i.e., as Giddens suggests: the experience of authority at work, the division of labour, and patterns of consumption (Giddens, 1982, p. 160). Giddens also stresses the role of 'the distribution of mobility chances which pertain within a given society' (Giddens, 1982, p. 159). Interestingly, Giddens notes that the greater the degree of 'closure' of such mobility opportunities, the more this encourages the development of classes as social groups, for this has the effect 'to provide for the reproduction of common life experience over the generations; and this homogenisation of experience is reinforced to the degree to which the individual's movement within the labour market is confined to occupations which generate a similar range of material outcomes' (Giddens, 1982, p. 159).

This too should sound familiar. Admittedly Giddens is discussing *class* consciousness. But what this means basically, is that he is offering a classification of factors which may facilitate the development, among individuals concerned, of an awareness of shared interests which are in opposition to those of specified others (see above). Clearly this may occur on a class basis, or on a more partial and parochial basis — such as has been considered earlier. And it is interesting how this important suggestion lays particular emphasis on the closure of social relations, on exclusion, on demarcations between categories of people. For we too have noticed how this phenomena is essential to the structuring of social relations. And we shall see below how the achievement of closure and exclusion is an important strategy deployed by groups in their attempts to advance their interests. In these cases, however, social closure is an element of the phenomenon, rather than a determinant of it. But in fact, like other key processes, it seems to be both a determinant of the development of shared interests, and a consequence of shared interests: we shall come across this again: there is an interaction between aspects and causes of group consciousness. For example, in both case studies, the shared culture and morality of the protagonists was a consequence of elements in their situations, as explained, but it also served to perpetuate their opposition and their homogeneity by legitimating it, and by defining the relevant outsiders in negative terms.

Giddens's classificaion of factors responsible for the structuration of classes, which we have borrowed in order to investigate the development of occupational or class consciousness, identifies those factors which generate common experiences. These experiences then influence the development of consciousness of interests. But for people to share an experience they have to see it in the same way; experience implies shared perceptions. As Giddens remarks, the *visibility* of shared situations and experiences is crucial. But, clearly visibility depends not only on the object, but on the viewer. In fact Giddens and other writers sensibly warn against a crude objective/subjective differentiation. For classes, or other work groups or occupations, to be structured into identifiable social groupings involves, as we have seen, consciousness and awareness, to some degree, for it is members of the groupings who define themselves as sharing a significant membership. Furthermore, once a work group of whatever sort starts to act in some manner in pursuit or defence of interests, such action itself both expresses shared interests and recreates them. Sabel, for example, notes: 'the members of the work group learn through collective experience how to realise their ambitions; and it is only as they begin to realise their ambitions that they discover what they really want' (Sabel, 1982, p. 188).

But if, in practice, the objective and subjective become merged, this is not to suggest that material factors are irrelevant: they are necessary but not sufficient. What is also important is a conception of their importance. Interestingly, it is possible that the sorts of factors mentioned in the earlier section as leading to the development of occupational communities, or to a sense of shared identity on a work basis, are also important in developing the necessary social basis for shared interests to be identified.

Certainly it is not true that location within the division of labour determines a worker's political vision, in the grand or the local sense. We must also consider the worker's expectations. And it is to a consideration of sources of variation in expectations that we now turn.

(3) Similiar experiences are a necessary but not a sufficient basis for the development of the 'visibility' of these experiences. In the first section of this chapter we considered those factors which are responsible for the development of occupational communities, and noted that these essentially involved conditions which (a) encourage the development of internal group solidarity while (b) encouraging a sense of estrangement from outsiders. Within the space mapped by these parameters, insiders develop a distinctive, shared culture which represents in moralized, symbolic and 'factual' form the solidarity and isolation of insiders. In this section Gidden's work has been used to describe the conditions under which these groupings are likely not simply to share a social world, but to define this in terms of conflicts of interest, to a degree which can usefully be described as consciousness of some sort. We have then isolated two types of determinants: those responsible for the development of social closure and exclusion (plus an associated legitimating culture), and those responsible for the development of consciousness among such groups. Such consciousness of interests can be of varying degrees of intensity, and is by no means an inevitable feature of socially demarcated work groups. The fracturing of workplace relations *is* associated with the three essential, elements described elsewhere and in the previous section (identity, culture and relationships) and involves a *potential* basis (of solidarity, exclusion an estrangement) for the development of a degree of opposition of varying sorts, but not *necessarily* with the development of a consciousness of shared interests.

In fact the development of such consciousness is also dependent on factors which (a) separate people from others and (b) establish a degree of commonality within, and differentiation without. Prime among these, for Giddens, is the distribution of mobility chances which is the main way in which social experience is demarcated and generationally reproduced. This is the highest level of social closure, as it were, and it is within the patterns of similarity and differentiation mapped by the structuring of mobility opportunities that the other key factors identified by Giddens (see below) have effect. The overlapping of patterns of mobility restriction and shared market-based experiences creates a potent mixture. It differentiates an experience that is simply happening to you as an individual from experiences that are seen as typical for people like us.

As Giddens notes, for this to lead to an awareness of shared interests to a degree which can be described as consciousness, requires that the shared life of insiders be clearly structured by market capacity such that the common, differentiating situation is clearly *experienced* as stemming from, and reflecting, economic circumstances and economic capacity and resources. As noted in the first chapter, Giddens identifies three key factors: the division of labour at work, relations of control, and patterns of consumption. These are significant to the degree that they fragment and consolidate relationships, and thus establish socially identifiable and distinct homogeneous social groupings, based not simply on shared experience, but shared experience of a particular, market-generated, sort. But clearly we cannot treat actors' perceptions and definitions of their experiences as givens. Even under the conditions which might be regarded as 'appropriate', actors insist on relying on their own definitions of their interests and expectations rather than the sociologits'. There are a number of conditions which have been identified as critically influencing peoples' expectations.

First, as many writers have noted, workers are not just or simply workers. Consequently there is always the possibility that a person's other, non-work roles may in some way structure his or her expectations of, or attitudes towards, work. For example, in a recent study, Thompson and Bannon note that the impact of job de-skilling will vary with the expectations of the workers involved. There are two ways in which jobs can be de-skilled. One way is to change people's jobs; the other way is to change the job *and* the people. The latter way is less disruptive, less likely to occasion resentment and resistance:

> the erosion of skills is not felt or experienced in the same way by the various sections of the workforce, or even by individuals. Long-time workers clearly had different criteria for judging the new technology than those with less experience, and felt the changes with a sharp sense of loss . . . . In contrast, while newly recruited workers at Huyton are bored by the reduced job demands, their responses are not governed by a feeling of loss of skills. (Thompson and Bannon, 1985, pp. 111–112)

In this case, the key variable determining reaction to de-skilling is length of work experience. Other writers have identified other intervening factors. Sabel for example, notes the role of social and geographical background:

> workers standing side by side in a factory do not necessarily view their work in the same way. Ghetto workers, would-be craftsman, and peasant workers, each with their own set of aspirations, might

be working on the same assembly line. In the same factory craftsman with downgraded skills and would-be craftsmen climbing the skill hierarchy might be adjusting the same machines, but judging the job in the light of diverse ideas of a career at work.' (Sabel, 1982, p. 187)

Studies of women workers support our basic thesis, by demonstrating that women's dual role as houseworkers and employees often tends to encourage women not to see their paid employment as a central life interest. Similarly the realities of the domestic responsibilities causes women to seek work which is compatible with these responsibilities, which in turn structure their attitudes towards, and expectations of, work. (Yeandle, 1985).

We would expect work expectations — which in turn will effect the 'visibility' of work conditions — to be structured by key social identities: gender, race, age, class. Furthermore, if we take an historical dimension, then individual's work careers and biographies will play an important role, as the remarks of Sabel above, suggest. To conclude this section on occupational studies. We have noted that within this tradition, occupations are identified as conscious, political phenomena, and we considered some of the explanatory advantages of this approach. However it was noted that the degree of consciousness of an occupation or work group could not be assumed, and indeed that this was itself an important area of investigation. In the later part of the section we considered some key issues raised by analyses of the determinants of consciousness. From the point of view of the two case studies discussed in the earlier chapters it was noted that neither were occupations, and that neither offered an example of full-blooded consciousness but both were examples of a lesser and probably more common order of interest consciousness: partial, incomplete resentment, expressed largely through the construction of negative information about the targeted outsider group, and the distrust of their pronouncements. In both cases conflict was expressed (and perpetuated) through the manipulation, distribution, construction and denial, of knowledge and information. In both cases interests were defined not as totally distinct and opposed, but as partially differentiated and opposed, partially similiar and shared. In these cases we are faced with examples of work-based social groupings centred on the three key elements described earlier: relationships, identity, and shared culture bounded by social boundaries of exclusion and inclusion, wherein a *degree* of interest identification and opposition occurs, but not to the extent that is identified by the type of studies considered in this section. In these cases the development of consciousness of the sort identified by Giddens has not occurred, and the determinants of such consciousness identified by Giddens are not present.

Certainly the station officers and the parties to the Moonidih modernization saw 'us' as sharing interests which were different from and sometimes opposed to those of 'them'. But this definition of interests was not in terms of market, and economic, forces and processes. It was rare for anyone to assert that the differentiated parties differed in terms of economic interest. The differences were defined in terms of organizational loyalties, cultures, career advantage, world-view, personal characteristics. We have now considered some of the factors responsible for the development of solidaristic, work-based groupings, and some of the factors responsible for the development of conceptions of shared interests. We shall now turn attention to a factor hitherto untreated: the *capacity* of groups to achieve their interests once they have agreed that they hold them in common. We shall consider this through a discussion of studies of internal organizational processes.

WORK GROUPS IN ORGANIZATIONAL SETTINGS

So far our analysis has focused on what occurs when work relations are so fractured as to generate patterns of internal solidarity and identification allied to external estrangement and opposition, and on the relationship between this phenomenon and the development of a consciousness of shared interests (to some, variable degree), or to the preparedness to act in their furtherance — or defence. In fact we have noted that the development of full-blown consciousness of interests, of the sort described by Krause and Giddens, is rare. What is more common is a lower order form of opposition. Even when work relations are so patterned as to give rise to the distinctive structures of solidarity and opposition described earlier, it is clear that this only rarely related to the *experience* of shared interests, and the *determination* to act to advance them.

Certainly this structuring of work relations axiomatically gives rise to the 'them' and 'us' level of solidarity and identification and estrangement from others so clearly displayed in both case studies. Certainly this is a potential base for the development of the level of work consciousness described by Krause. But in the majority of cases 'them' and 'us' consciousness does *not* lead to explicit group-organized opposition. The differentiation and fracturing of workplace relations of the sort of concern in this book is most usually related to a low level but pervasive form of opposition and conflict — at least as far as action is concerned.

So far our analysis has touched upon but has not developed an important element of any oppositional relationship. We have considered the origins of this relationship, and the factors which play a part in the development of consciousness of shared interests. But we have not considered *capacity*. Our analysis has occurred in the language of interests, centring around the question: under what circumstances do those social patterns develop which in turn develop an awareness of shared and opposed interests? It is this question which constitutes the subject matter of this section.

We have already noted that *forms* and *levels* of opposition vary greatly. Indeed despite the talk, within the labour process debate, and within that tradition of occupational sociology, of occupations, or work groups acting politically, to advance their shared interests through *strategies* (which carry the impression of organized and far-sighted steps in pursuit of goals), our own case studies offer a less developed form of action. Indeed in a sense they offer no *action* at all. In both cases what they offer is *words*. Opposition is conducted at the level of language talk, muttering, gossip, theory. In the case of station officers, this took the form of a language which was heavily emotional. The language and the sentiments which it both reflected and encouraged was violent, emotional. In the case of the modernization of Moonidih, protagonists' language lacked this emotional element. Nevertheless it clearly carried and demonstrated, an 'oppositional rhetoric'. Whereas in the first case the language referred explicitly to, and focused on, the opposition of interests between senior management and the watch, and supplied examples of this opposition, and explained it in terms of senior management's careerism; in the second case the language although apparently rational and analytic, and indeed sometimes formalized in reports, nevertheless revealed a major rift between two opposing theories, each of which identified different aspects of the problem, and questioning the other's competence or integrity. In both cases, language reflected its origin in structural differentiation and opposition, albeit in different degrees and to different intensity.

But in both cases the opposition thus revealed was taken no further than words. Words reveal opposition, and encourages opposition and it is by words that opposition is operationalized. These two elements of revelation and operationalization overlap closely, yet remain separate.

For example, in the case of Moonidih there is little operationalized, concrete, opposition; yet the fact that the parties to the modernization programme hold opposed views of it, and of why it is not successful, in itself constitutes a barrier between them (and this opposition of views in itself arises from, we have argued the asymmetric relationship between the parties involved). However, this difference of viewpoint is not actively and purposively exploited. In fact members of both groups are more trapped within their rhetorics than they are active exploiters of them.

In the case of the station officers, on the other hand, we find the officers actively seeking to emphasize their differences; not just living within them, but promulgating them, celebrating them, seeking converts, insisting on rigid adherence to the sacred canons of their position, creatively embellishing them. In a sense they are as imprisoned within their rhetoric as the people involved in the Moonidih project. But for the station officers theirs is an imprisonment which they revel in and wish actively to perpetuate.

The station officers seek to emphasize their difference from senior management, and insist on defining this difference, in terms of their superior, moral commitment to the goals of the organization. The station officers actively select and mischievously try to undermine the EO programme, insist on the untrustworthiness of those who offer alternative conceptions of the programme, or its effects.

But it is more than the *forms* of opposition which vary (and which usually do not even approximate to the fully developed conscious strategies described in the literature) it is also the capacity of groups to act in terms of their opposition. From organizational sociology come numerous studies of work groups within work organizations which supply an important and hitherto missing element to our unfolding analysis, for these studies move beyond the determinants and elements of work-based structuring of relationships, and the origins of work-based consciousness of shared interests, to a consideration of the problem of *capacity* — to the question of the power of groups to act in furtherance of their interests, as well as their willingness to do so.

Let us begin with some examples of the sort of studies we are concerned with. Roy (1973) reports on his experiences working on unskilled, highly repetitive factory work. The work was 'a grim process of fighting the clock . . . . I had struggled through many dreary rounds with the minutes and hours during the various phases of my industrial experience, but never had I been confronted with such a dismal combination of working conditions as the extra-long workday, the infinitesimal cerebral excitation, and the extreme limitation of physical movement' (Roy, 1973, p. 208). Around him, Roy gradually discerned 'occasional flurries of horseplay so simple and unvarying in pattern and so childish in quality that they made no strong bid for attention' (Roy, 1973, p. 208). Gradually, however, his perception of these activities altered and he began to appreciate them for what they were: rituals, games, with known and accepted rules, expectations, roles and routines — temporal patterning of horseplay, joking, familiarity, seriousness, which succeeded in introducing an element of enjoyment of communication for its own sake, in opening up a world of caricature and banter which was so well known as to require no work, and which was fun to participate in.

The temporal dimension was particularly important. The routines fragmented the formal work periods, offering predictable breaks: recognizable occasions for the performance of identifiable and well-rehearsed episodes of banter, hinging around some aspect or action or preference, grossly caricatured, of a member of the work group. Roy emphasizes two implications of these episodes. First they involved distinctive patterning — achieved through regulation, enforcement, expectation, however gentle, of non-work topics and themes. The predictability and patterning were constructed, not fortuitous. 'From these interactions may also be abstracted a social structure of statuses and roles' (Roy, 1973, p. 218). Secondly, Roy argues that these patterns of informal banter had a consequence. They were fun, and while this probably had minimal consequences for output, it may have affected labour turnover, since it constituted a method of dealing with the 'beast of monotony'.

Studies of informal practices in police organizations in Amsterdam and 'Skid Row' in urban USA, also offer some useful insights into the nature, causes and consequences of informal work group structuring within employing organizations. Both studies considered here (Bittner, 1973; Punch, 1985) stress the ambiguities, or duality of police work — enforcing the law versus keeping the peace. Indeed even enforcing the law can lead to tensions between short-time and long-term considerations. Furthermore, for police to be effective they need to relate to, and to a degree live in, and 'know' the area or community they police. Their success, survival and efficiency can easily be experienced as depending on the 'flexible' interpretation of the law in particular cases in order to achieve a general and continuing effectiveness in the light of what is known about the person or about 'people like that'. The law then can become a strategy, a resource, rather than a source of clear and unvarying practice. Bittner, for example, shows through many examples, how, in the light of their 'knowledge' of characters and moralities on skid row, patrolmen 'often make decisions based on reasons that the law probably does not recognise as valid' (Bittner, 1973, p. 336).

Bittner reports that peace-keeping on skid-row consists of three elements:

> Patrolmen seek to acquire a rich body of concrete knowledge about people by cultivating personal acquaintance with as many residents as possible. They tend to proceed against persons mainly on the basis of perceived risk, rather than on the basis of culpability. And they are more interested in reducing the agregate total of troubles in the area than in evaluating individual cases according to merit. (Bittner, 1973, p. 343)

These elements constitute a clear work-group culture. The 'knowledge' is specific to the patrolemen on skid row duty; officers who deviate from the rules — for example by amplifying disturbances through 'excessive' violence — are discouraged, or moved, and those who enforce the law naively are similarly tutored in the consequences of such inflexibility. Bittner's analysis explains patrolmen's practices largely in terms of the exigencies of the work demands as the patrolmen see them: 'those procedures and considerations that skid-row patrolmen regard as necessary, proper, and efficient relative to the circumstances in which they are employed' (Bittner, 1973, p. 344).

Bittner's analysis usefully shows that police work, like other sorts of work, involves informal structuring in ways which deviate from formal requirements, and which make use of established police 'knowledge' of typical suspects, victims, criminals — of different types — in the light of what are regarded as the 'real' or 'proper' objectives and priorities of the work, all in the context of the need to ensure continuing effectiveness within a context of criminality (or constant potential criminality). From inside such a culture, the rules, strongly enforced by the group of which the police officer is a member, a group on which s/he may depend for his or her survival, and certainly for continuing efficiency, seem sensible, even proper. From outside, they may seem to be evidence of corruption and malpractice. This is the focus of Punch's study of the Amsterdam police.

Punch's study rejects the pervasive view of police corruption — the rotten apple theory whereby corruption and malpractice are conveniently attributed to individuals, who are thus individually discovered, prosecuted and punished, leaving the systemic origins of such practices untouched. Like Bittner, Punch sees the origins of what can be seen from outside as corruption in the fact that police organizations are not integrated and harmonious but deeply divided, differentiated, and semi-autonomous. Secondly, definitions of 'real' police work, and of proper objectives and priorities differ from formal, official ones, often owing more to what is perceived as street realities than official or political or legal requirements. And thirdly, police use the law as a resource, a strategy, a bargaining counter in their attempts to resolve practical dilemmas. Out of these elements develops the constant systematic likelihood of corruption.

In this view, police corruption becomes an 'understandable' response to what are experienced as work problems and dilemmas, in view of the shared knowledge and assumption among police officers. In much the same way the viewpoints of the participants in the two case studies are sensible in the light of their 'knowledge' and evaluation of their situations — as they see them. The station officers resist the EO programme not because they are necessarily personally corrupt, but because it threatens their interests in their conception of how the job is and should be. But the analysis must be taken further.

Of critical importance to the development and persistence of 'informal' organizational practices (which in the case of police officers may also be illegal practices) is the structure of power within the organization. How does police 'deviance' or disobedience relate to formal authority? First, as Punch remarks, although police organizations manifest many of the trappings of tight authority and regulation, this is misleading. Evidence from studies of police behaviour report frequent malpractice and rule-infringement (Smith, 1983). Police can evade and break the organizational rules to which they are formally subject, like other workers. Furthermore senior officers may implicitly condone 'shop-floor' deviance, so long as it does not get out of hand. Senior officers may accept that the practical realities of police work require a degree of discretion, of horse-trading, of breaking the law to enforce the law, of using prevalent police knowledge and practice in the face of the exigences of the street. Or they may accept that various formal requirements and restrictions on police officers' behaviour are in practice unworkable or irrelevant or just silly. Indeed research suggests that malpractices are so common it is impossible not to infer that they must be at least condoned by senior management.

Punch notes that a retired Commissioner of the Metropolitan Police has written of rule-bending within the police that it occurs for what the ex-commissioner describes as 'perfectly honourable reasons', as methods of combating biases in the justice system.

Equally, despite the evidence of the Policy Studies Institute of systematic racism within the Metropolitan Police, legislation introduced in April 1985, making it an offence for a police officer to stop, search, arrest, threaten, assault or improperly treat a person because of his/her race, colour or ethnic origin, by Christmas 1985 not one officer had been charged with the new offence — an obvious boycott of the regulation.

The informal culture of police officers is further greatly strengthened by the power of group ties. Studies of police officers all stress the importance of solidarity and secrecy. Police officers, like members of other tight-knit groups, do not inform on each other. Although the behaviour current within the group may, to outsiders, seem deviant and corrupt, within the group, the major form of deviance is informing on, and thus betraying, the group. Such solidarity and secrecy support each other, by emphasizing the officers' separateness, and strangeness, from outsiders. But these mechanisms also work against informing *within* the organization, for example by betraying a fellow officer to senior officers. Punch describes the informal culture as an 'introspective culture, which approaches the structure of a secret society, is powerful, swiftly encapsulates newcomers, condones occupational deviance, and can be punitive if the 'rule of silence' is broken and solidarity is threatened' (Punch, 1985, p. 121). Within the code, behaviour externally regarded as deviant and as malpractice is seen as normal, reasonable, necessary.

The case of police officers' informal codes and structures is no different essentially, in nature, from other more humdrum examples of informal structuring. We may, as citizens, feel that it matters more. And we may also argue that when the rules that are flouted are not simply bureaucratic requirements but laws, then deviance is no loner an internal matter. Nevertheless the studies by Bittner and Punch both emphasize that the basis of the informal structuring is the same as in more conventional industrial settings.

Roethlisberger and Dickson's 1930s study of the Hawthorne plant of the Western Electric Company signalled for many the 'discovery' of the existence, nature, and consequences of informal structuring of work-based relationships (Roethlisberger and Dickson, 1964). The researchers considered the internal organization of workers in the department, with a view to identifying patterns of membership, exclusion, loyalty. Meticulous records were kept of patterns of banter, associations, popularity, joking, even regular arguments. On the basis of this material, the researchers conclude that the workers were not integrated on the basis of occupation. However, 'every record examined seemed to be telling something about these configurations. Whether the investigators looked at games, job trading, quarrels over the windows, or friendships and antagonisms, two groups seemed to stand out' (Roethlisberger and Dickson, 1964, p. 508). The existence of these groups is of interest, anticipating Roy's argument, that the apparently random, inconsequential, sometimes foolish and even childish, usually highly repetitive world of workplace banter and exchange is in fact an organized, structured social world of systematic relations, values and social control. Roethlisberger and Dickson in stressing the structuring aspect of informal patterns of relations in the department, identify the *objects* of such control, as well as its general existence. They note the *prescriptive* character of workplace relations, and note the impact of such prescriptions for work behaviour. When considering levels of work output, the researchers noted that: 'In considering the output of the members of the group it is necessary, first of all, to recall their general attitude toward output. It has been shown that the official 'bogey' meant nothing to the operators. In its stead they had an informal standard of a day's work which functioned for the group as a norm of conduct, as a social code. They felt that it was wrong to exceed this standard' (Roethlisberger and Dickson, 1964, p. 517). These standards of work performance and output were enforced by and within the group, in the same way that attitudes towards the EO programme and senior officers' statement about it were controlled and applied within the London Fire Brigade. Workers who complied with the norms were highly regarded. Those who deviated were punished, through sarcasm, ridicule. There was a link between compliance with group norms and status within the group, between social standing and output. The low-status deviant was someone who broke the group's norms, but prestigious obedience to these conventions meant, in effect, rejecting the company's requirements.

Interestingly Roethlisberger and Dickson appreciate the control implications of informal work structures. When seeking to understand the 'functions' of the phenomenon, they argue: 'The social organization of the bank wiremen performed a twofold function: (1) to protect the group from internal indiscretions, and (2) to protect it from outside interference . . . nearly all the activities of this group may be looked upon as methods of controlling the behaviour of its members' (Roethlisberger and Dickson, 1964, pp. 523–524). A feature of this control of outsiders was that any supervisor or inspector who attempted to intervene too grossly in the group's work arrangements or rhythms, and who attempted to reject group autonomy could be undermined by the group putting in excessively large daywork claims, which supervision was meant to limit. Internal control over members' work output was argued by the practitioners themselves in terms of fears about the dangers of the rate per unit of output being reduced, or the wage/effort exchange being modified in management's favour. The researchers themselves preferred a more anodyne explanation which would seem, however, to incorporate the workers' view: the function of the group norms was to resist change. But a particular type of change was involved: changes introduced by 'specialist technologists' which would have had consequences for the content of workers' job (de-skilling), for their status, for their work satisfaction, for their pay rates, for their levels of activity. Quaintly, Roethlisberger and Dickson, are unable to define these consequences as evidence of any essential conflict of interest between worker and management. They go to great lengths to insist that workers' insistence that their economic interests are threatened by management, and by the specialist technologists, are simply delusions: 'the ideology expressed by the employees was not based upon a logical appraisal of their situation and . . . they were not acting strictly in accordance with their economic interest' (Roethlisberger and Dickson, 1964, p. 534). Nevertheless even if, in Roethlisberger and Dickson's paradigm, there can be no logical conflict of economic interest between worker and management, the consequence of the technologists' proposals for employees' jobs and working conditions was regarded by the workers themselves as something to be resisted 'the technologist may be unwittingly a source of interference and constraint. Resistance to such interference was the chief external function of the bank wiremen's informal organization' (Roethlisberger and Dickson, 1964, p. 547).

These three cases of informal work structuring supply us with the possibility of generating some general points about the development, nature and consequences of such structures within organizational settings, which, in turn, will allow us to develop our analyses of the two case studies. We shall organize these generalizations under three headings: what is this informal structuring *of*, and how is it maintained? How do they relate to formal structures of power and control? And what determines the capacity of informal groups to achieve or defend their interest?

(1) What is this informal structuring of?

The three cases support our earlier examination and consideration of the London firemen and the modernization of Moonidih. The informal structuring of relationships at work involves, to differing degrees, three interrelated elements: identity, patterns of exclusion and inclusion of social relationships (Strongly argued by Roethlisberger and Dickson, who actually chart the nature and frequency of social contacts, and on this basis were able to delineate the contours of patterned sociability), and values. The three elements interrelated in that, as the examples from Punch and Bittner demonstrate, members conform with the norms with which they live and work because, from within the world of the sub-culture, they make sense. They describe the world, and offer working routines with which to deal with it. If these differ from formal requirements, or even from the law, that is simply an unfortunate cost of the insiders' privileged and isolating predicament. But such a marked separation of insider from outsider makes the fact of fellow-members' support even more necessary. This closely supports the analysis of both case studies where we argued that participants were indeed closely involved in what they themselves insisted were separate and meaningful structures of delineated relationships and their associated bodies of knowledge and morality. But our cases varied noticeably in the degree of intensity of such structuring.

So members comply, because the norms make sense to them from where they stand; it's simply natural. And compliance brings the admiration and esteem of fellows, who think in the same way; and association with these like-minded fellows supports self-image and the culture it internalizes.

(2) Relationship with formal structures of power and control

The cases above, and the case studies described earlier, demonstrate a variable relationship to formal authority. In the case described by Roy it is possible to argue that the practices, culture and group control developed had little relationship with, and few consequences for, management control and foremen's authority. Largely on the basis of this study Katz has argued that informal work groups develop in the 'space', the areas of autonomy permitted within the formal structure. According to this perspective informal structures are not in opposition to, but are complementary to formal authority, which they work to support.

Within work organizations, argues Katz, there is always some degree of autonomy — some areas where control is not applied. 'There is therefore scope for the development of various informal patterns: some patterns lessen the boredom of workers and in other ways help get work down; others are contrary to the goals of the organisation' (Katz, 1973, p. 191). Overall, however, Katz argues that the development of such structures assists the survival and integration of work organizations. Katz sees the existence of informal structures as means whereby formal authority wins, or manipulates the integration of those involved, into the organization as a whole. 'Blue-collar' workers are integrated into the workplace by being, as it were allowed space to develop, to a limited degree, their own groupings and cultures which permit the importing of characteristically working-class cultural elements. Katz describes this as a form of managerial federalism. However, the cases reported by Punch, Bittner, and Roethlisberger and Dickson suggest another interpretation, one implied by the last two researchers: that informal structuring can be a form of *resistance* to formal authority. But this possibility must be qualified.

First, it is clear that a major element in the sort of structures we have considered in this book is the incorporation of first line management in the loyalties and culture of the work group. This is evident in the case of the police, and our analysis of station officers in the LFB. Other studies of this phenomenon confirm this occurrence: first line management finds that it is more comfortable, more sensible and, from their point of view more effective, to follow the code of the group than of the formal hierarchy.

Secondly, there are undoubtedly occasions when senior management too, at least tacitly, condones the culture and practices of the informal groupings. This can then be inflated and legitimized as a conscious strategy of management; or it can be implicitly condoned but formally sanctioned. In short, there are certainly cases where the informal culture and practices not only flourish, but establish a sort of underground legitimacy. Senior management may be prepared to accept such activities in exchange for a degree of workforce goodwill. Or this situation may even be regarded as a conscious management strategy.

However, the work of Roethlisberger and Dickson suggests at least the possibility of a more directly confrontational relationship between management authority and informal structures of workplace relationships, although interestingly, none of the researchers whose work has been mentioned chooses to develop this possibility. To a degree this unwillingness to recognize the potential of informal structures for opposition and resistance reflects the researchers' theoretical leanings. Roethlisberger and Dickson, in particular, seem almost obsessively concerned to reject the view that any logical oppositon of economic interest could occur between management and shop-floor. But just as important as the researchers' theoretical preferences is the fact that, although overt opposition between employees and management may occur along the lines of informal structuring, in fact this opposition (a) is not an inevitable outcome, (b) is likely to take a relatively passive form, as discussed earlier, and (c) is likely to cover some particular issues of major significance to the group's perceived interests, rather than to constitute total, all-out rejection of management authority.

Such highly partial and sectional conflicts can indeed be seen as evidence of issue-based conflicts which could well have the consequence of integrating the resisters into the total fabric of the organization. Certainly it is not safe to assume that such conflict — resistance to changes which could negatively affect the group's interests — is necessarily evidence of an overall rejection of management authority. In fact by enabling powerful sub-groups to mobilize and achieve their sectional interests, such struggles may well reduce the likelihood of a more radical confrontation.

At the same time, such resistance — of whatever intensity and form — is obviously of considerable potential importance for the introduction of programmes of change. To argue that it is not necesarily *class* resistance is not to argue that it is therefore of no significance, except in an excessively Bravermanic form of approach.

This issue takes us to the heart of a central problem within the sociology work, and indeed, sociology as a whole, one identified in the first chapter: the structuration of classes, and class strategies. A major problem within sociological theory is the complex and unpredictable (or, at least, unpredicted) relationship between class structures as delineated in terms of economic intrests, and social categories with a consciousness of themselves and their shared, class interests. This problem — of class 'structuration', and the determinants of class consciousness and class action — was identified in the first chapter. It was there noted that solutions to the problem required an understanding of the causes and ways in which 'classes' were fractured by their situations and experiences. One approach to the lack of 'fit' between class as a theoretical category and class as an axis of lived group experience has been to discover how theoretical classes are in fact differentiated and divided, by their social or economic situations or even by deliberate management strategy.

It has, for example, been argued by 'radical theorists' as Rubery sensibly calls them, that 'divisions in the labour market are artificial, imposed by capitalists to counter the homogenisation of the labour force and thus prevent the development of class opposition' (Rubery, 1978, p. 24). Foster's study of class consciousness in Oldham in the nineteenth century also argues that the development of a 'labour aristocracy' composed of a segment of production workers who were delegated authority over the rest, fragmented worker consciousness and solidarity (Foster, 1974).

However, this thesis has to be treated with caution. Certainly, it is necessary to investigate management strategies of each and every sort; certainly a 'divide and rule' tactic is apparent — not least as a clear feature of industrial relations tactics; certainly a factor in management attitudes towards restructuring and job design or rationalization is the effect on work attitudes and subjectively. But it must also be remembered that job differentiation can have advantages for workers too, and that the initiative may come from, and be supported by, them. As Rubery argues it is too often assumed that 'the development of a homogenous labour force would maximize the benefit to workers and the disadvantage to capitalists' (Rubery, 1978, p. 21). However, Rubery points out that in fact the development of capitalism, and work technologies has had a more complex effect than this simple proposition suggests. Capitalists are faced with more than the problem of blocking the development of class consciousness. They also have to organize the social relations of production effectively, productively and and profitably. Workers will indeed react to the threatened introduction of a new technology by seeking to protect their knowledge and skill; management must take such resistance into account, and 'cost' it. Further, workers will attempt to control entry into their work. These strategies, Rubery notes, will segment the labour market, by barring certain categories of workers from entry, and controlling access. But these strategies also

> provide shelter from labour market competition for the incumbent workforce . . . the existence of a structured labour force, where jobs are strictly defined, and workers are not interchangeable, provides a bargaining base for labour against management's attempts to increase productivity and introduce new technology. Changes in job ladders, skill demarcations and the pace of work become areas for bargaining, whereas a homogeneous labour

force, interchangeable in function, would lay itself open not only to competition from the external market but also to further declines in workers' control of production and a continuous undermining of bargaining power. (Rubery, 1978, p. 29)

A major strategy for sub-group power and resistance is thus to protect the skill base — the work 'mystery' — when this is possible. A useful way in which this can be done is through *exclusion*: control over (and limits on) entry into the occupation, group, or unit; control over the distribution of work within the group (who does what and what qualifications are required). These strategies, when successful, serve to construct and preserve skill, through retaining a monopoly over the knowledge — and access to it — within the group. The mechanisms by which workers seek to preserve their positions and interest, when successful, also serve to differentiate the class overall. Penn, for example, argues that craft forms of resistance to mechanization centre around

mechanisms of social exclusion. More precisely, skilled manual workers in mechanised factory milieux are defined by their high degree of social control over the operation and utilisation of machinery. These exclusive controls involve a double exclusion, both of management from direct or complete control over the labour process and of other workers who offer a potential threat to such controls. (Penn, 1985, p. 121)

(3) The determinants of sub-group's power

The complexity of this issue has been noted in the earlier sections. One major problem is that a group's strength is increased by its consciousness of itself as a group and its determination to act to defend shared interests. Consciousness, strategy, mobilization are themselves sources of strength. But there are limits to this. For a group to be successful requires more than mere consciousness. Its strategies must also be successful. History is littered with forgotten and unsuccessful efforts to resist occupational de-skilling or debasement. Resisters must also have resources which they can deploy, trade, bargain with.

Our analysis may be assisted by a distinction between strategy and capacity. The distinction is not always a clear one. But it is a start. Strategies are conscious and considered attempts to increase the capacity — the bargaining power — of a group or a collection of workmates. Capacity refers to those features of a group's position or activities — those resources — which allow it to escape threatened changes, or give it privileged position in the distribution of rewards. Pettigrew, using the work of E. P. Thompson on the attempts by nineteenth century craftsmen to resist technological change confirms our discussion above and notes that such groups tried to protect the knowledge base of their skills through the apprentice system, as well as becoming politically involved. Pettigrew's analysis of struggles for status and rewards among computer personnel demonstrates that the specialist groups did indeed seek to protect their knowledge base, through denying the competence of the newcomers, developing myths which comforted fellow workers by supporting their notions of the importance — and mysteriousness — of their unique skills and attitudes; seeking to hold, manipulate, restrict information which could be used to reduce the uncertainty or mysteriousness of their work. Pettigrew notes that many other studies (including that of Roethlisberger and Dickson) also show that groups seeking to protect their position seek to retain autonomy by making outside interference impossible by restricting the flow of information about their work processes. We have already noted the importance of strategies of exclusion. Summarizing the literature on this strategy, Freedman argues:

> In the labour market, maximising group interest and minimising risk rests on the exclusion, which may be justified on the grounds that people are not members of certain associations, that they lack credentials or seniority, or that their age, sex, or race is inappropriate. Whatever the particular exclusionary mode, the purpose is to constitute barriers to entry into preferred occupations. (Freedman, 1984, p. 57)

These strategies are sensible. There is considerable evidence that the power of a sub-group within an organization is a function of its control over certainty. Indeed such control over uncertainty is probably what 'skill' actually means in a particular setting. This control may be achieved deliberately through the deployment of strategies. But once achieved it yields real power. Of course more groups wish to achieve such control than actually manage to obtain it. A clear statement of the basis of sub-unit power within an employing organization has been provided by Hickson and McCullough (1980). They write that the power (capacity) of a unit or group within a organization stems from that group's capacity to cope with what are critical organizational problems:

> But not just any problem. Most power potentially derives from those problems about which there is greatest uncertainty. A problem to which there is a ready answer is not a source of differential power. But a subunit which can cope with uncertainty

will gain in power . . . the theory argues that a subunit will be most powerful if it copes effectively with high uncertainty, is non-substitutable, and is central both in terms of immediacy and of pervasiveness. (Hickson and McCullough, 1980, pp. 41, 43)

The same principle, of advantages accruing to coping with uncertainty, can be seen to hold on an organizational level. Senior members of modern work organizations value staff who are responsible, reliable, committed. It has been suggested that in order to encourage these attitudes key personnel may be permitted jobs with, relatively, 'primary employment conditions' — good pay, security, good conditions. Garnsey *et al.* argue that whether jobs attract these 'primary' features or not is determined by

differences in employers' capacity to tolerate relatively fixed wage costs and to evade uncertainty. In brief, strategies for coping with economic uncertainties structure the demand for labour and play an important part in determining whether primary or secondary type employment conditions are provided by employers. Wherever possible, employers providing primary employment conditions attempt to pass the costs and burdens of uncertainty on to smaller firms on a subcontract basis or by setting up satellites, while concentrating production and service provision in areas where demand is reasonably stable and predictable. (Garnsey *et al.*, 1985, p. 56)

Struggles between groups or aggregates of workers which occur across lines of social fracturing — between groups of people who share some sort of work life together — thus demonstrate a complex relationship with class structuration. Clearly these struggles for sectional advantage can not in themselves be seen as displays of class solidarity. Indeed it could be argued that by their attempts, sectionally, to protect and defend subunit interests and skills, workers actually fragment class solidarity. But, such struggles can, in a larger sense, be seen as *products* of class dynamics, as management seeks constantly to reorganize production in terms of increased profit and competitiveness; and those workers who can seek to resist this dynamic in the only ways available to them — through their particular and precarious control over some scarce organizational resources, i.e. access to activities which bestow some control over organizational problems. There is also a further connection between such struggles — and the strategies they frequently involve — and class structures in the widest sense. The quotation from Freedman given above indicates that exclusion strategies often involve attempts to exploit pre-existing social categories of low esteem, or low social prestige and power — the old, women, minority ethnic groups, immigrants, children. Existing social divisions can readily be used by groups seeking to shift some of the likely costs of organizational and technical change. It is for this reason that the most vulnerable workers are most likely to be found in low-paid jobs. 'The bargaining position of these workers is limited by factors not affecting the majority of the labour force, such as ill-health, household responsibilities, alien nationality, minority racial status, lack of employment experience or a combination of these factors' (Garnnsey *et al.,* 1985, p. 5).

SUMMARY

In this chapter we have come on a long journey. *En route* connections with the case studies have been made, but there is still a need to pull together the implications of the analysis in this chapter for the case studies, and the implications of the case studies for this analysis. We shall do this in the final chapter. Essentially in this chapter we have rehearsed the various ways in which different traditions within the general area of the sociology of work have addressed the subject matter of the book. Three major traditions were considered: occupational communities; studies of occupations as political entities; and sub-groups or informal structures within organizational settings. It will have been noted that these traditions overlapped considerably. But each contributed a distinctive focus. The first identified the essential elements of a particularly intense version of our phenomenon — the occupational community — and considered some of the conditions under which these develop. The second identified the conditions under which occupations, or other collections of people who worked together, could develop a consciousness of shared interests and a preparedness to act in pursuit of them. The third considered some classic studies of informal groupings within employing organizations, identified the main elements of such structures, and analysed the strategies such groupings could deploy to advance or protect their interests. Finally, some connections with class analysis were briefly sketched.

5

Conclusion

In the beginning we extolled the advantages that could accrue if we could start again afresh ignoring the current preoccupations and predilections of the mid-1980s sociology of work, and re-establishing the issues and approaches that a hypothetically bereft sociology would offer. Of course this was largely rhetoric; the point was simply to try to escape the burden of current debates, but in so doing to escape to other debates. In fact the preceeding chapter has shown how the subject-matter of this book is a major focus of the various sociologies of work. But it was not entirely rhetoric. Current 'problems' within industrial sociology (the 'labour process') and the theories which both account for and produce them, are severely limited. In Chapter 1 it was argued that even in their own terms, labour process theories are unable to account for their own, selected problems (the design of work, and the role of class priorities and dynamics within work organizations) without incorporating an understanding of, and an approach to, the ways in which work organizations were fractured and differentiated. These patternings of internal social relationships, it was suggested, play a significant part in the mediating of the levels of consciousness and understanding which must be required to produce the management strategies — and the responses — which Bravermania and its adherents, are concerned with.

But this was argued largely to introduce our subject matter, certainly not to exhaust its interest. Indeed Chapter 1 also argued that there are more interesting sociological questions to ask of, and problems to resolve in, work than Bravermania and the labour process dream of. And if we are to make progress with these wider questions which are not initially, and many are not ultimately, to do with class, we require an understanding of, and an approach to, and a taxonomy of, forms of structuring of work relations.

And at this point in the argument, because it was felt that the reader, however well-disposed to the argument, might be beginning to experience an appetite for concrete illustration of the form and advantages of the approach, we then included discussion of the two cases. In most ways they couldn't be more different; but is some respects, it was argued, they were similar. In both cases there were programmes of planned change — the introduction of an Equal Opportunities programme within the London Fire Brigade and the installation of powered faces on longwall panels in Moonidih, BCCL. In both cases there were problems with the change: resistance to the programme, and slow progress, poor output from the powered faces. And in both cases, it was argued, resistance to, or disappointing results from, the programmes of change were structurally generated in the existence of patterns of organizational relationships. In the case of the station officers, it was argued that a number of factors co-existed and coalesced to separate station officers and members of the watch from senior management, and to structure communications between these two collectivities in terms of mutual distrust. Furthermore, since station officers had built their personal self-images at least partially on their work role, their resistance to a programme of change which also undermined their traditional influence over recruitment and selection was consequently exacerbated. Station officers had seen themselves as an elite — a small proportion of those who applied were successful, membership had been won painfully as they demonstrated to their seniors and the themselves that they were of the right stuff — they could take the humiliations, the hosings, the constant banter, the ridicule of their seniors. And when they were replaced by another 'junior buck', then they would make sure that the new recruit got as much as they ever had. But this pride in work and work indentity was undermined by a policy which, as they saw, outlawed the systematic humiliation of recruits (for this could now be sexism of racism), opened up recruitment to previously ineligible groups, wrested control of recruitment and selection from the stations and the Brigade and placed it in the hands of 'professionals', and actively sought to encourage, equip and qualify those who would otherwise not have applied or not have succeeded in their applications.

Our analysis suggested that the Equal Opportunities programme, however rational, moral, and proper, because it threatened station officers' interests and identities, and bacause of the role of the informal separation of station officers from upper management, met with considerable resistance.

In the case of Moonidih, there can be little doubt that real difficulties do still exist in the installation and transfer of new coal cutting technology. In Chapter 3 it was not argued that the problems *originated* in patterns of work relationships, identities and loyalties. But is was suggested that the poor capacity of the complete system, including suppliers and manufacturers and consultants and CIL and Moonidih management, to learn and correct in the face of acknowledged difficulties, was exacerbated by the ways in which this total system was fractured in a series of overlapping ways, so that owners of the problem were separated from owners of expertise, givers from receivers, clients from consultants. A major consequence of this was the polarization of explanations of the poor results, which in their turn, obstructed further improvement. We did not seek in that chapter to offer an account of the origins of the disappointing output. That will be done elsewhere. It is also certainly an organizational problem, and the key features of the organization which obstruct adjustment to new technology are the form and degree of centralization, and the individual insecurity which managers experience in a management system which encourages caution, and can penalize innovation. But that is another story.

At Moonidih, it was argued, an essential and important process of technical modernization was being hampered by the way in which the roles and responsibilities and perspectives and interests of those involved were systematically but inadvertently differentiated. This was enough to establish two opposed conceptions and explanations of the problem.

Furthermore, in both cases, the symptoms of the problem were similar, although different in degree. In both cases the problem was articulated in words, language, theories, accounts. In neither case did any of the parties do anything but discuss, communicate, explain. Thus were the differences aired, and amplified. In both cases the symptom of the problem — theories, accounts, 'knowledge', work moralities, myths, etc., were also the problem itself. And in both cases these ways of knowing and explaining derived from the manner in which relationships within the organization were structured into patterns of exclusion–inclusion, trust–distrust, identification–estrangement.

And finally in both cases, these patterns derived not from formal design and organization, but from informal processes. In both cases the major lines of fracture (for our phenomenon consists essentially of boundaries, demarcations, differentiations) derive from the experience of similarity and of shared interests, in contrast to differences and opposed interests. In both cases these patterns of similarity versus difference were inadvertent: they were fortuitous consequences of formal structure and processes, on the basis of which developed distinctive patterns of 'endogamous' socializing, an insider culture and identity. But, interesting as these cases may be, we cannot leave it at that. If, as was suggested, the fracturing and patterning of workplace relations is not only a significant, practical issue but a major concern of the sociology of work, then it is clearly necessary to consider what sociology has to say on this issue. And Chapter 4 represented an effort to review the relevant literatures. Three major contributions were considered there: work as a basis of community, occupations as interest groups, and informal groupings within employing organizations. These analysis overlapped considerably but each also offered a distinctive contribution, and a contribution which could be applied to the two cases considered earlier.

The Firemen, for example, can be seen in terms of the three component elements of an occupational community (relationships, culture and identity). The origins of this community probably lie in the sorts of factors usually responsible for the development of these phenomena.

The protagonists in the Moonidih programme do not constitute an occupational community, although some parts of the complete system — for example the miners themselves — certainly do. But overall there is not one community here incorporating Coal India, BCCL, Moonidih, etc. However, this example demonstrates that even a much less dramatic and intense form of structuring of work relationships and identities can be significant. The various parties of each 'side' in this project are themselves differentiated — in the UK the manufacturers, BMC, the ODA personnel etc. Nevertheless there was much greater consistency of viewpoint within each 'side' than there was between the two sides; and more differences between them than there were within.

This relatively low level of structuring was not caused by the factors responsible for the development of occupational communities. It was caused by the clustering and overlapping of different sorts of relationship to the shared problem, which allowed the gradual accretion of contrasting and ultimately mutually opposed explanations.

The analysis of occupations as interest groups also helped our understanding of the case studies. First, it was immediately apparent that in neither case could the groups concerned be regarded as conscious interest groups in the sense described by Krause and Giddens. Nevertheless in both cases, there was a *degree* of consciousness of shared interests, but this (a) was far short of full-blown consciousness of separate and *opposed* interests, and (b) was not associated with a determination of preparedness to act in furtherance of these interests. The sense of opposition was partial, and situational. It concerned some issues but not all, or even not many. It did not involve any preparedness to resist the targeted outsider totally, but only specifically. And the resistance as noted, took the form of mere words, or more accurately, the construction of stories, gossip, rumour, anecdote, explanation; the construction of facts, theories and moralities. But these mere words were most significant.

Furthermore the section in interests groups introduced the discussion of strategies, via a brief consideration of professions, and the way in which successful claimants of professional status always deploy various strategies, including obtaining control over access to the work, the mystification of the skill/knowledge base, and the mobilization of ideologies insisting that the professional practitioner (licensed of course) is alone able to identify and achieve the public good. The final section of the previous chapter considered various cases of informal structures and groups at work. It was noted how these involved a degree of internal control, which was then enforced on members, and that compliance with group views and moralities brought popularity and status. Such conformity is all the more likely in that it makes sense in view of shared knowledge about work, workmates, clients, bosses. This discussion also introduced the question of power; of the relationship between the control of some subunit or work group over its members and the control of the formal hierarchy over the subunit. At least potentially, the existence of a structure of work relations in patterns of exclusion–inclusion, identity–estrangement etc., represents a threat to formal control in that, as Roethlisberger and Dickson noted, such structures offer internal discipline and solidarity, and external strength. As the studies demonstrated, they often co-exist with an incorporated supervision, and with the tacit approval of middle management. At the same time there is nothing inevitable about this, and they may be the basis from which opposition to formal authority occurs. However, it should be noted that for some writers, the type of informal structures under consideration in this book represent a basis for the incorporation of the group in the total collectivity. This can occur, it has been argued, because the activities, and games and routines of the sub-group represent a source of distraction, thus making the intolerable bearable. Similarly, but more subtly, Burawoy (1979) has argued that the types of negotiation often characteristic at the interface of sub-group and formal authority — negotiations which are game-like in their predictability and rule-boundedness — can also serve to protect the organization as a whole by allowing relatively unimportant bargaining to take place and thus legitimize the overall structure of authority and hierarchy.

Interestingly our analysis of the relationship between structures of work relationships and power within the organization led us back to where we began — to class and questions of class structuration. Because the structuring of work relationships involves the differentiation and 'fracturing' of collections of workers or employees, it represents a factor in the development, or lack of development, of overall class consciousness — a basis on which employees can or cannot develop conceptions of shared identity and shared interests. We have seen that the very essence of the phenomenon we are dealing with is a degree of internal solidarity and external exclusiveness. The degree varies, as the two cases illustrate. Solidarity and exclusion constitute bases for the development, or the fracturing, of wider class consciousness. In fact in the vast majority of cases they represent barriers to class solidarity, since the axis on which differentiation occurs is sectional, not class-based.

But at the same time solidarity and exclusion are possible bases for resistance to, or evidence of, central organizational authority. We have seen that the form and focus of this resistance varies greatly, as do the issues on which resistance occurs. But informal structures of work relations are always potential bases for power and resistance, which centre around protecting or advancing what are seen as shared interests. As such, this informal power and organization can be seen as representing, or leading to, or fracturing, resistance to management's class-derived initiatives, and thus as examples of class resistance. But again while this is a possibility, the very sectionalism of the majority of most examples of such struggles makes it an unlikely development.

Formal work organizations, as we noted in Chapter 1, involve the deliberate purposive structuring of work activities and work roles. In theory this structuring is based on the application of what is regarded currently as rational, systematic and effective; but in practice many negotiated, political, factors are also relevant. What this book has argued is that formal differentiation and re-integration of work organizations inevitably sets up axes along which informal differentiations and integrations will take place. It is not possible or necessary to try to specify exactly which axes these will be, or where such structuring will occur to be able to assert that they will emerge, somewhere. It is almost as if the attempt, 'rationally' and formally to design and structure work paradoxically achieves a shadow structuring, inadvertent and unexpected. The exact role and implications of this shadow structuring will also vary, but it will always constitute at least a potential rival to formal views and intentions. And it will play a significant role in any attempt to introduce change for, as this book has tried to show, the shadow structures are, for those who live within them, the source of work identity, work knowledge, morality and significant relationships. As such they are a basis for resistance, opposition, distraction, incorporation. They are therefore key elements in managerial attempts to achieve control.

This book has centred around an analysis of two case studies. We have sought to argue that analysis of this type, which identifies and seeks to understand and explain patterns of informal structuring of workplace

relations, is important as a method of understanding organizational structure, process and dynamics. It is thus an essential element in any form of
sociological enquiry into work organizations.

Currently fashionable forms of sociology of work (the Labour Process)
demonstrates an interest in, and a theoretical focus on, the design of work,
and the role of class factors (dynamics) and relationships in the determination of organization design, technology, and organizational structure. It
is not, therefore, particularly concerned with informal patterns of relationships. Yet it should be. For since the Labour Process is increasingly
required to temper the simplicity of Braverman's thesis with the ornamen-
tation of qualification, it finds it necessary to draw upon (or assume)
concepts such as strategy, resistance, consciousness which can only develop
within a context of actors' (or agents') conceptions of, feelings about, and
objectives of, their work. Once this is granted the Labour Process, and
indeed any other form of sociology of work must take seriously, and
investigate, the ways in which employees' world of meaning, understanding
and evaluation are in fact constructed.

This short book is an effort to encourage this enterprise of discovery. It
has been argued that a major determinant of actual worlds of work meaning
is the informal structuring of work relationships, which in the majority of
cases is not organized on a class basis, although it may be amenable to a
class-based analysis and explanation.

And so it has been argued that the systematic analysis of the ways in
which (and consequences of) the structuring of work relationships, is
relevant even within that tradition which is most clearly uninterested in it.
But it is even more relevant to a more general sociological interest in
organizational structure and process, particularly process — our analyses
have both demonstrated how programmes of planned change run into pre-
existing, or somehow themselves help to generate, forms and degrees of
resistance which revolve around axes of social differentiation between
change agents and those on whom the changes will have impact.

The axes on which such demarcations occur vary, as we have seen. They
arise out of the inadvertent construction of perceived interest, whereby
formal structures or formal programmes somehow construct, or allow
space for the development of, informal distinctions and structures of
expulsion/inclusion, trust/distrust, shared meanings / opposed or different
bodies of meaning. These structures of demarcated homogeneity are
particularly significant when they collide with programmes of planned
change.

On this ground, given a perception of change or threat to existing
practices, to 'us' and our preferences and philosophies, 'they' assume their
destined role in the mythology of the group, as outsiders, strangers, threats

— barbarians. We have frequently noted that the key expression of the phenomena under analysis here is the act of expression itself; language. The divisions we are considering live in language and are effective through language; the language of 'them' and 'us' with their associated bodies of knowledge and mortality and mythology. And the most striking feature of this language, which we have incorporated in our discussion too, when we talk of 'them' and 'us', is precisely its polarization — its reference to a series of binary distinctions; 'us' and 'them'; good and bad, trustworthy and untrustworthy, sympathetic, unsympathetic, loyal, traitor, etc. The pheno-menon we are dealing with here expresses itself in language with the same binary mode, between the two poles of which there is the same sort of relationship, as it reveals in its social organization; inclusion, exclusion; insider; outsider. The strength of resistance to, or feeling towards, or contempt for, the outsider is a function of the constructed homogeneity of the insiders. The exclusive groups needs the excluded outsiders; they depend on them, indeed in a sense they create them. But not entirely, for the construction of internal solidarity and its product—external opposition or alienation — is also encouraged by structural factors which separate and conjoin interests, as the case of the station officers shows. In a sense this book and its approach, are about the rationality of organizations. In the beginning of sociological interest in large-scale organizations, Weber's notion of rationality was a useful and influential concept on which models of bureaucracy were based. And although it was soon noted that in practice actual organizational structures and events were constructed around other criteria, the formal significance of rationality was retained as something towards which organizational decision-making strived, at least in theory. But in sociological theory Weberian rationality was soon replaced by marxist rationality, i.e. the imperatives and constraints of the market, profit, competitive advantage, or, on the other hand, solidarity, resistance and class consciousness.

Within the Labour Process tradition, actors were omniscient, conscious strategists, aware of, and responding to, the rationalities of Marxist analyses of work organizations within capitalism. Obviously, however, in fact, actors — members of these organizations — were no more rational in this sense than they had been in the previous Weberian sense. In both cases it is necessary to explore the development and construction and content of employees' rationalities rather than simply to assume and assert them. And if this injunction is taken seriously then, we have suggested, it is necessary to explore the complex ways in which the construction of patterns of social inclusion and exclusion constitute the basis of the lived reality of work.

Bibliography

REFERENCES

Albrow, Martin (1970) *Bureaucracy*, Macmillan, London.

Armstrong, Peter (1984) 'Competition between the Organised Professions and the Evolution of Management Control Strategies', in Thompson Kenneth (ed.), *Work, Employment and Unemployment*, The Open University Press, Milton Keynes, pp. 97–120.

Bittner, Egon (1973) 'The Police on Skid Row: A Study of Peace-Keeping', in Salaman, Graeme, and Thompson, Kenneth (eds.), *People and Organisations*, Longman, London, pp. 331–345.

Braverman, Harry (1974) *Labor and Monopoly Capital*, Monthly Review Press, New York.

BMC (British Mining Consultants) 'First Stage of Operational Assistance for the Dowtry Mechanised Longwall Faces at Moonidih Colliery, BCCL'.

BMC (British Mining Consultants) (1983) 'Operational Assistance Mechanised Longwall Mines, Coal Sector, India'.

BMC (British Mining Consultants) (1984) 'Mechanised Longwall Planning Assistance for Coal India Ltd'.

Brown, Richard (1984) 'Working on Work', *Sociology*, **18**, pp. 311–325.

Burawoy, Michael (1979) *Manufacturing Consent*, University of Chicago Press, Chicago.

Child, John (1973) 'Organisational Structure, Environment and Performance: the Role of Strategic Choice', in Salaman, Graeme, and Thompson, Kenneth (eds.), *People and Organisations*, Longman, London, pp. 91–107.

Cohen, Sheila (1986) 'Labour Process and Class Consciousness', Ph.D. dissertation, Open University.

Cottrell, W. F. (1940) *The Railroader*, Standford University Press.

Dennis, Norman, Henriques, Fernando, and Slaughter, Clifford (1956) *Coal Is Our Life*, Eyre & Spottiswoode, London.

Dunkerley, David and Salaman Graeme (1986) *Key Problems in Industrial Sociology*, Polity, Oxford.

Edwards, Richard (1979) *Contested Terrain*, Heinemann, London.

Elliott, Philip (1975) 'Professional Ideology and Social Situation', in Esland, Geoff, and Salaman, Graeme (eds.), *People and Work*, Holmes McDougall, Edinburgh, pp. 275–286.

Expert Group (1984) 'Report of the Expert Group on Powered Support Longwall Faces in India'.

Financial Times (1984) 'Mining Gets a Move On', 11 June.

Foster, John (1974) *Class Struggle and the Industrial Revolution*, Methuen, London.

Freedman, Marcia (1984) 'The Search for Shelters', in Thompson, Kenneth (ed.), *Work, Employment and Unemployment*, The Open Univresity Press Milton Keynes, pp. 55–66.

Garnsey, Elizabeth, Rubery, Jill, and Wilkinson, Frank (1985) 'Labour Market Structure and Work-force Divisions', in Deem, Rosemary and Salaman, Graeme (eds.), *Work, Culture and Society*, The Open University Press, Milton Keynes, pp. 40–76.

Giddens, Anthony (1980) 'Class Structuration and Class Consciousness', in Giddens, Anthony, and Held, David (eds.), *Classes, Power and Conflict*, pp. 157–174.

Giddens, Anthony (1982) 'Power, the Dialectic of Control and Class Structuration', in Giddens, Anthony, and Mackenzie, Gavin (eds.), *Social Class and the Division of Labour*, Cambridge University Press,

Cambridge, pp. 29–45.

Gouldner, Alvin (1954) *Patterns of Industrial Bureaucracy*, Free Press, New York.

Greater London Council (1982) 'Report to Public Services and Fire Brigade Committee of the Study Group'.

Hickson, David and McCullough, Arthur, F. (1980) 'Power in Organisations', Salaman, Graeme and Thompson, Kenneth (eds.), *Control and Ideology in Organisations*, The Open University Press, Milton Keynes, pp. 27–55.

Homans, George (1961) *Social Behaviour: Its Elementary Forms*, Routledge & Kegan Paul, London.

Katz, Fred, E. (1973) 'Integrative and Adaptive Uses of Autonomy: Worker Autonomy in Factories', in Salaman, Graeme, and Thompson, Kenneth (eds), *People and Organisations*, Longman, London, pp. 190–204.

Krause, E. A. (1971) *The Sociology of Occupations*, Little, Brown Co., Boston.

Littler, Craig, R. (1982) *The Development of the Labour Process in Capitalist Societies: A Comparative Analysis of Work Organisation in Britain, the USA, and Japan*, Heinemann, London.

Littler, Craig, R., and Salaman, Graeme (1984) *Class at Work*, Batsford, London.

Lockwood, David (1975) 'Sources of Variation in Working Class Images of Society', in Esland, Geoff, and Salaman, Graeme, and Speakman, Mary-Anne (eds.), *People and Work*, Holmes McDougall, Edinburgh, pp. 197–208.

Marx, Karl (1974) *Capital: A Critical Analysis of Capitalist Production*, Lawrence and Wishart, London.

McKinlay, John, B. (1973) 'On the Professional Regulation of Change', in Halmos, Paul (ed.), *Professionalisation and Social Change*, University of Keele, Keele, pp. 61–84.

Penn, Roger (1985) *Skilled Workers in the Class Structure*, Cambridge University Press, Cambridge.

Perkins, Kenneth, Blake (1984) 'Causes of Occupational Communities: A Theoretical Study of Occupational Solidarity in Contemporary Society', Ph.D. Dissertation submitted to Virginia Polytechnic Institute.

Pettigrew, Andrew (1975) 'Occupational Specialisation as an Emerging Process', in Esland, Geoff, Salaman, Graeme, and Speakman Mary-Anne (eds.), *People and Work*, Holmes McDougall, Edinburgh, pp. 275–286.

Punch, Maurice (1985) *Conduct Unbecoming*, Tavistock, London.

Roethlisberger, F. J., and Dickson, William (1964) *Management and the Worker*, Wiley, New York.

Roy, Donald (1973) 'Banana Time: Job Satisfaction, and Informal Interaction', in Salaman, Graeme and Thompson Kenneth (eds.), *People and Organisations*, Longman, London, pp. 205–222.

Rubery, Jill (1978) 'Structured Labour Markets, Worker Organisation, and Low Pay', *Cambridge Journal of Economics*, 2, pp. 17–36.

Sabel, Charles, F. (1982) *Work and Politics*, Cambridge University Press, Cambridge.

Salaman, Graeme (1974) *Community and Occupation*, Cambridge University Press, Cambridge.

Salaman, Graeme (1979) *Work Organisations, Resistance and Control*, Longman, London.

Salaman, Graeme (1982) 'Managing the Frontier of Control' in Giddens, Anthony and Mackenzie, Gavin (eds.), *Social Class and the Division of Labour,* Cambridge University Press, Cambridge, pp. 46–62.

Silverman, David (1970) *The Theory of Organisations,* Heinemann, London.

Smith, D. J. (1983) *Police and People in London, vol 3. A Survey of Police Officers,* Policy studies Institute, London.

Taylor, Robert (1982) *Workers and the New Depression*, Macmillan, London.

Thompson, Paul (1975) *The Nature of Work*, Macmillan, London.

Thompson, Paul, and Bannon, Eddie (1985) *Working the System*, Pluto Press, London.

Tunstall, Jeremy (1969) *The Fishermen*, Routledge & Kegan Paul, London.

Yeandle, Susan (1)84) *Women's Working Lives*, Tavistock, London.

Weber, Max (1964) *The Theory of Social and Economic Organisation,* Free Press, New York.

Wood, Stephen (ed.) (1982) *The Degradation of Work*, Hutchinson, London.

FURTHER READING

Eldridge, J. E. T. (1976) *Sociology and Industrial Life*, Nelson, Middlesex.

An unusual, and useful summary of some major issues in the sociology of work, and their origins in classic sociology theory. Wide ranging and individual, the book not only presents new insights into the work of the early theorists but also relates these to a wide selection of current empirical developments. Refreshingly, it offers a much broader range of theoretical issues than are addressed by current forms of theory.

Burawoy, Michael, (1979), *Manufacturing Consent*, University of Chicago Press, Chicago.

Drawing upon, but developing, Roy's earlier analysis of informal shop floor structures, Burawoy develops a theory of the nature and role of such structures in the negotiated construction of the degree of workforce consent necessary in any form of work organization. Burawoy's book thus represents an attempt to address the subject matter of this volume, and to incorporate it within a theory of class control and its contradictions.

Littler, Craig, and Salaman, Graeme (1984) *Class at Work*, Batsford, London.

Although in general within the Labour Process debate, this book focuses on the way in which class pressures and dynamics are translated, at work, in contradictory requirements for control and consent which are expressed in oscillating tendencies of work design — from Taylorism to Work Enrichment.

Salaman, Graeme, and Thompson, Kenneth (ed.) *People and Organisations*, Longman, London.

A selection of accounts of life and work within employing organizations. The selection covers the issues discussed in this volume — i.e. the actual ways in which organizational life is structured and differentiated and constructed, 'informally'. It includes many articles which are used in the present volume.

Index